101 EASY TEST INSTRUMENT PROJECTS

BY ROBERT M. BROWN & TOM KNEITEL

TAB BOOKS Inc.
BLUE RIDGE SUMMIT, PA. 17214

FIRST EDITION

FIRST PRINTING

JANUARY—1981

Copyright © 1981 by TAB BOOKS, Inc.

Printed in the United States of America

Reproduction or publication of the content in any manner, without express permission of the publisher, is prohibited. No liability is assumed with respect to the use of the information herein.

Library of Congress Cataloging in Publication Data

Brown, Robert Michael, 1943-
   101 easy test instrument projects.

   Includes index.
   1. Electronic instruments—Design and construction—Amateurs' manuals. I. Kneitel, Thomas S., joint author.
II. Title.
TK9965.B743   1980   681'.2   80-27702
ISBN 0-8306-9619-9
ISBN 0-8306-1339-0 (pbk.)

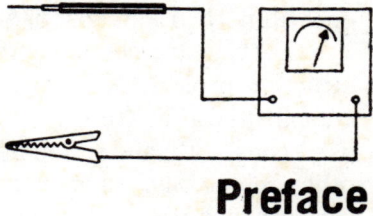

Preface

Every electronics hobbyist—regardless of individual "specialty"—needs reliable test instruments. Too many of us, however, do not have the expense account required to set up a truly efficient, all-encompassing array of these costly gadgets. So we make a few of our own. We combine circuits, take parts from ancient projects, and hope for the best.

This book is a random gathering of the finest measurement and testing devices that can be built for a minimum cash outlay. The key word is "minimum." Perhaps we should say "cheap."

With few exceptions, these are strictly one-evening projects guaranteed to please, both in performance and in cash outlay. Most can be assembled entirely from parts that you may already have on hand. If you lack a healthy supply of component parts, however, you can purchase them commercially from any reputable electronics parts distributor. In many cases, you will find your entire bill amounting to well under $10.00!

To help you along, a substitution guide has been included in Appendix A. Further, you may feel fairly safe in substituting other components not crucial to circuit performance. This would not be true of, say, a resistor bank governing a meter readout; this you would not want to alter for fear of distorting calibration. Capacitors are generally safe within reason. If you do not have a .0022 μF, try a .002, .0015, .003, or even a .001. If your electrolytic capacitor is not exactly on the button, do not chuck the project. In some instances where the circuit calls for, say, a 10 μF, 150 Vdcw electrolytic, a 12 μF, 250 Vdcw will be satisfactory. Similarly, just because we used a 15k potentiometer doesn't mean a 20- or even 25k pot will not work almost as well.

Test instruments represent the ultimate in a construction project. Not because they are necessarily more complicated—far from it—but primarily because they are used constantly and relied upon in checking performance of other electronic (and nonelectronic) units. For these reasons, you will want your finished project to be ruggedly housed, well wired, and (if a meter is involved) well calibrated. All wiring should be short and to the point. All possible causes for internal shorts should be checked prior to putting an instrument into service. Good solid solder joints contribute heavily to most equipment successes. Check yours over meticulously. If your project includes a battery (self-contained), check it frequently to prevent deterioration and ultimate corrosion.

Note: The electronic parts numbers listed in this book are intended only as a guide in selecting the correct types of electronic components.

The reader is referred to the many electronic substitution guides, such as the "Archer Semiconductor Guide", available at Radio Shack.

Enough lecturing—on to the projects!

Robert M. Brown
Tom Kneitel

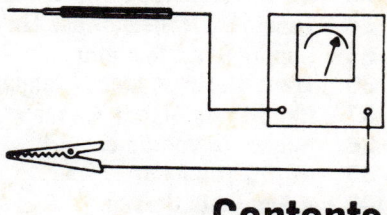

Contents

1	Shockless Continuity Tester	9
2	A Tester's Sinewave Generator	10
3	Household Handy Wattmeter	12
4	Novel VOM Range Expander	13
5	Dry Cell Rejuvenator	14
6	Transistor Variable Power Supply	16
7	Homemade RF Probe	18
8	Inexpensive Impedance Checker	20
9	Experimenter's Power Supply	22
10	Ham's RF Meter	24
11	Line-Voltage Booster	26
12	Transistorized Moisturemeter	28
13	Neon-Lamp Tone Generator	30
14	Dynamic Mike for Testing	32
15	Transistor Experimenter's Power Supply	34
16	One-Tube Frequency Standard	36
17	Crystal Microphone Substitute	38
18	Electronic Timer	40
19	Intermediate Frequency Checker	42
20	Simple Astable Multivibrator	44
21	Ham's Audio Oscillator	46
22	VOM RF Indicator	48
23	High-Voltage Silicon Rectifier Checker	50
24	Diode RF Probe	52
25	One-Transistor CB Field Strength Meter	54

26	Dial-A-Volt Miniature Power Supply	56
27	Two-Transistor Sine-Wave Generator	58
28	Sound Level Meter	60
29	The $1.50 Signal Generator	62
30	Audio Frequency Meter	64
31	Frequency Meter/Monitor	66
32	Inexpensive Meter Sensitizer	68
33	Deluxe Transistor Signal Tracer	70
34	Tubeless, Transistorless Light Meter	72
35	Simple Short Detector	74
36	Transistor Frequency Standard	76
37	Neon-Lamp Signal Tracer	78
38	Miniature Voltmeter	80
39	AC-DC Voltmeter	82
40	A Small Multitester	84
41	Radio Frequency Calibrator	86
42	All-Around Multitester	88
43	Junk-Box Capacitor Tester	90
44	Flashlight Battery Rejuvenator	92
45	Multipurpose Comparator	94
46	Transistor Checker	96
47	Add A Signal-Strength Meter	98
48	Radio-TV Tube Rejuvenator	100
49	One-Transistor Signal Tracer	102
50	Handy Fuse Saver	104
51	Professional Dual-Meter Transistor Checker	106
52	Low-Voltage Silicon Rectifier Tester	108
53	Transistor Metronome	110
54	Flashlight Cell Tester/Charger	112
55	Filament-Type Tube Tester	114
56	Diode Frequency Meter	116
57	Miniature VOM	118
58	Capacitor Leakage Checker	120
59	World's Simplest SCR Checker	122
60	VOM Used to Indicate RF	124
61	Inexpensive 40-13,000 Audio Oscillator	126
62	Shop Interference Filter	128
63	Variable Output Transistorized Power Supply	130
64	Inexpensive Photo Relay	132
65	Footswitch Unit Controller	134
66	100 kHz Receiver Calibrator	136
67	High-Frequency Oscillator	138
68	Automatic Tool Magnetizer	140

69	Handy Vibrator Rejuvenator	142
70	Diode-Type CB Field Strength Meter	144
71	Simple Audio Tracer	146
72	Transistorized Square-Wave Generator	148
73	Transistor Signal-Injector Probe	150
74	DC Motor Supply Unit	152
75	Neon-Lamp Polarity Tester	154
76	108 MHz Receiver Calibrator	156
77	Filament Transformer Power Supply	158
78	Blown-Fuse Indicator	160
79	TV Picture Tube Rejuvenator	162
80	Versatile Crystal Oscillator	164
81	Two-Transistor Signal Generator	166
82	One-Transistor Dip Meter	168
83	RF Meter	170
84	One-Tube CB Q-Multiplier	172
85	In-Circuit Transistor Tester	174
86	Radiation Finder	176
87	Universal Two-Way Radio Tester	178
88	Tubeless Variable Frequency Oscillator	180
89	Simple Signal Tracer	182
90	Variable Bench-Voltage Supply	184
91	Transistorized Injector Probe	186
92	Grid Dipper Modulator	188
93	Simple Phase-Shift Oscillator	190
94	One-Tube Signal Injector	192
95	Direct Current Controller	193
96	Versatile $1.99 Tester	194
97	Metal Locator	196
98	Capacitor Tester for VOM's	198
99	High-Voltage Converter for Your Battery	200
100	Antenna Current Indicator	202
101	Universal Test Speaker	204
	Appendix A—Substitution Guide	206
	Appendix B—Resistor Color Codes	207
	Appendix C—Capacitor Color Codes	208
	Index	210

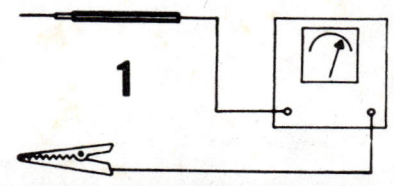

Shockless Continuity Tester

Here is a good starter for your test equipment projects. Its cost will be only a few cents, but with it you will be able to test for burned-out light bulbs, open filaments of tubes, fuses, and many other items around the home. See Fig. 1 and Table 1.

Use your ingenuity to make this as neat and small as possible.

Table 1. Parts List for Shockless Continuity Tester.

Item No.	Description
B1	1.5-volt flashlight battery.
M1	1.5-volt flashlight bulb.

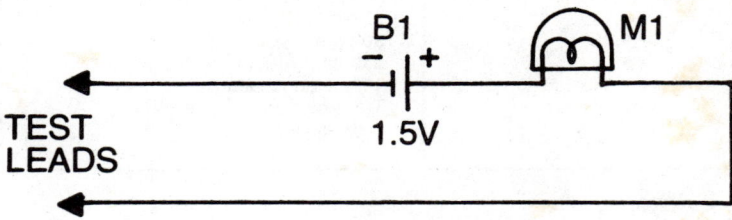

Fig. 1. Continuity tester circuit.

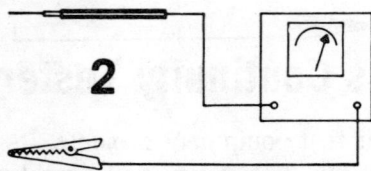

A Tester's Sine-Wave Generator

Sooner or later anyone who works on electronic equipment will need a good sine-wave generator. This one can be used for hi-fi testing, filter experiments, and testing modulators. With the components as shown, it generates a 2kHz signal.

Three output jacks are provided for low, medium, and high impedance outputs. A switch may be installed in the battery lead if desired. The battery drain is quite low. See Fig. 2 and Table 2.

Table 2. Parts List for Testers Sine-Wave Generator.

Item No.	Description
C1	.2-μF capacitor.
C2, C3, C4	.02 microfarad capacitors.
B1	9-volt battery.
M1, M2, M3	RCA phono jacks.
Q1, Q2	2N466 transistors.
R1, R2	30-ohm resistors.
R3	240-ohm resistor.
R4, R5	110k ohm resistors.
T1	Transistor transformer (Argonne AR-172 or equiv.).

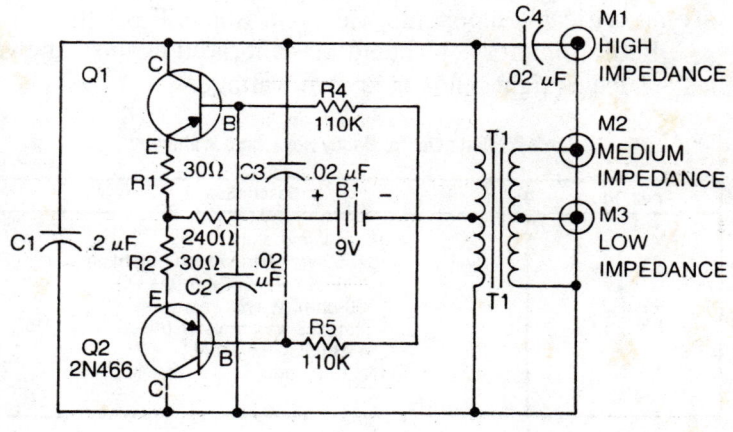

Fig. 2. Sine-wave generator circuit.

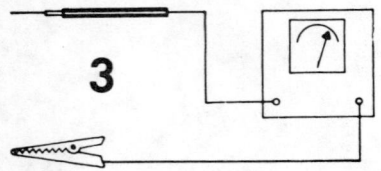

3

Handy Household Wattmeter

A wattmeter can be of considerable help in spotting electrical or electronic problems before they cause complete equipment breakdown. For instance, if a piece of equipment is consuming more power than the rated amount, it may be assumed that there are problems.

This is essentially a simple piece of test gear. There are no critical components. See Fig. 3 and Table 3.

Potentiometer R1 should be calibrated against known loads such as light bulbs of known wattage.

Table 3. Parts List for Handy Household Wattmeter.

Item No.	Description
M1	0-1 milliammeter.
R1	16k, 50-watt wirewound potentiometer (Ohmite No. 0327 or equiv.).
R2, R3	1000-ohm, ½-watt resistors.
R4	1-ohm, 25-watt resistor (Allied Radio No. 45B5203C or equiv.).
X1, X2	1N118 diode.

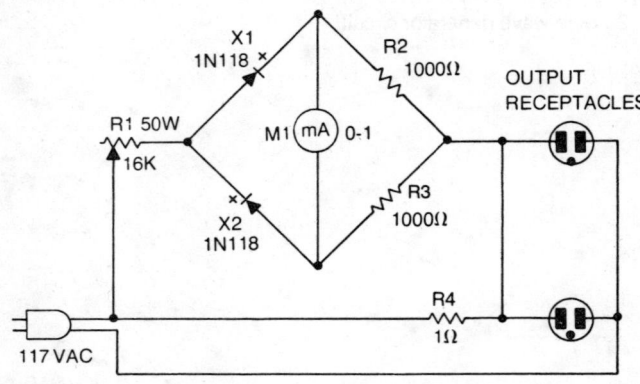

Fig. 3. Household wattmeter circuit.

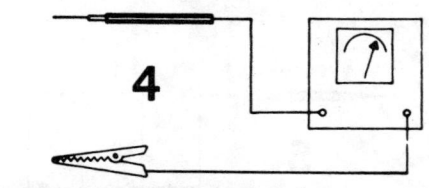

Novel VOM Range Expander

This simple circuit is a multiplier circuit that can be used with most VOM's having an R × 10,000 resistance range with a 12-ohm center-scale reading and an internal battery of 7.5 volts. By its use, the high-resistance scale is multiplied by ten. For instance, if the meter reads 120,000 ohms, you have a resistance of 1.2 megohms. See Fig. 4 and Table 4.

The advantage in using this multiplier is the added range it will provide. Set your VOM to its highest scale. Each reading is ×10.

Table 4. Parts List for Novel VOM Range Expander.

Item No.	Description
B1	67.5 volt battery.
R1	1.1meg resistor.

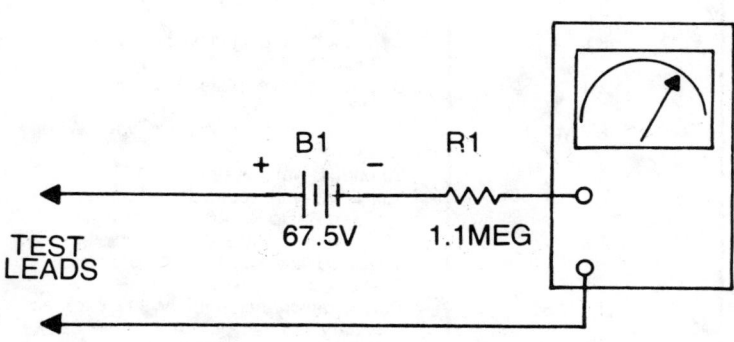

Fig. 4. VOM range expander circuit.

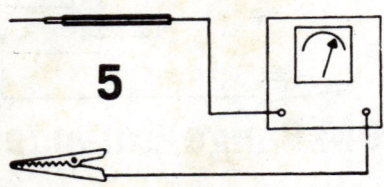

Dry Cell Rejuvenator

In the present era of transistorized equipment, batteries are used to supply power for small radios, children's toys, and a host of less well known items. Dry batteries can be recharged if care is taken to accomplish the process. Thus, a worthwhile saving can be made.

The unit described here will charge batteries ranging from 90 volts down to the more common 1.5-volt cells. The circuit provides positive protection against overloads and an excessive charging rate. The design shown here will permit a charging current of about 6 milliamperes. Beyond this figure the relay opens, lighting pilot light M2 and killing the charging circuit. See Fig. 5 and Table 5.

Table 5. Parts List for Dry Cell Rejuvenator.

Item No.	Description
C1	20-μF, 250-volt electrolytic capacitor.
C2	10-μF, 250-volt electrolytic capacitor.
F1	1-A fuse.
K1	Dpdt enclosed plug-in type relay (Allied Radio No. 41B5292 or equiv.).
M1	0-10mA dc meter (Allied Radio No. 52B7600 or equiv.).
M2,M3	6.3-volt pilot lights (Sylvania Type 6MB or equiv.).
R1	20-ohm, 2-watt resistor.
R2	15k, 5-watt wirewound potentiometer (Allied Radio No. 46B1119 or equiv.).
R3	10k, 5-watt wirewound potentiometer (Allied Radio No. 46B1118 or equiv.).
S1	Spst switch.
T1	Power transformer: primary, 117 Vac, secondary 125 Vac, 50 mA, 6.3 Vac, 2 mA (Allied Radio No. 54B1411 or equiv.).
X1,X2	Rectifiers (GE 504A or equiv.).

Use the Low and Common leads for charging batteries of up to 20 volts. Above 20 volts use the High and Common leads. Remember, to obtain longest life for your batteries, keep the charging rate low. Do not exceed 5 milliamperes even on the larger type batteries. Smaller batteries should have appropriately lower charging rates.

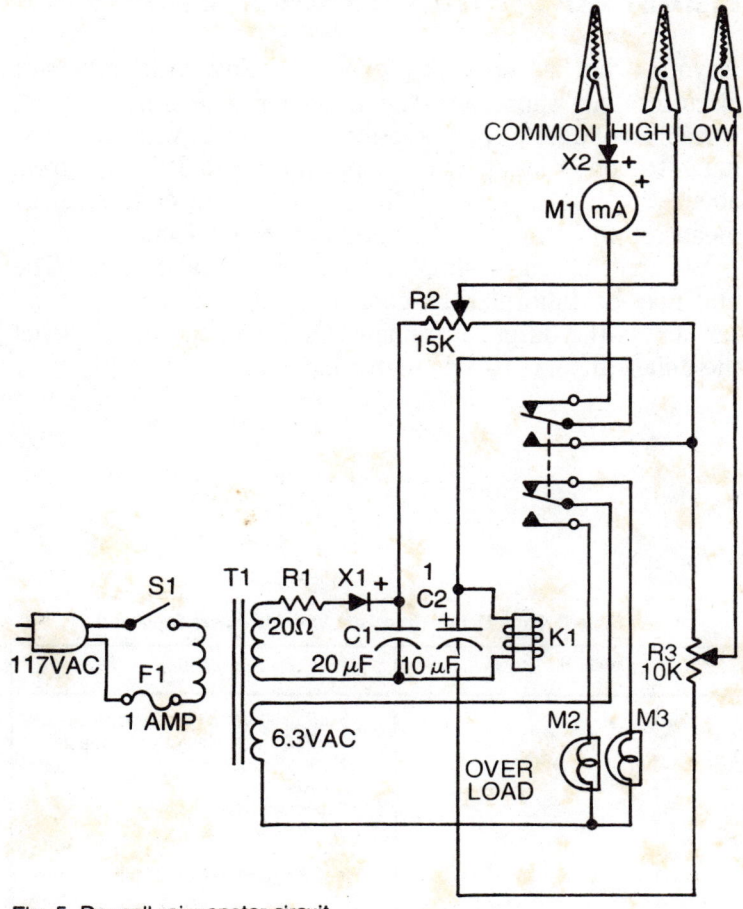

Fig. 5. Dry-cell rejuvenator circuit.

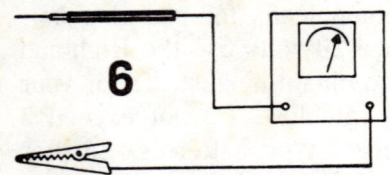

6

Transistor Variable Power Supply

Anyone who has done any experimenting with transistor circuitry will appreciate the need for a small, compact, variable-voltage power supply. This unit will not cost much to construct and can supply the needed voltage from about 1 volt to 9 volts. Voltage control, of course, is by means of potentiometer R2. See Fig. 6 and Table 6.

Construction is simple, with no critical factors. The unit may be calibrated by connecting a load and a voltmeter across the output terminals. Or, if you wish, construct the unit with an 0-10 Vdc meter included.

Table 6. Parts List for Transistor Variable Power Supply.

Item No.	Description
C1	15-μF, 150-volt electrolytic capacitor.
C2	20-μF, 25-volt electrolytic capacitor.
Q1	SK3004 transistor.
R1	1.1k resistor.
R2	15k Potentiometer.
R3	20k resistor.
R4	110k resistor.
X1	Rectifier (GE-504A or equiv.).

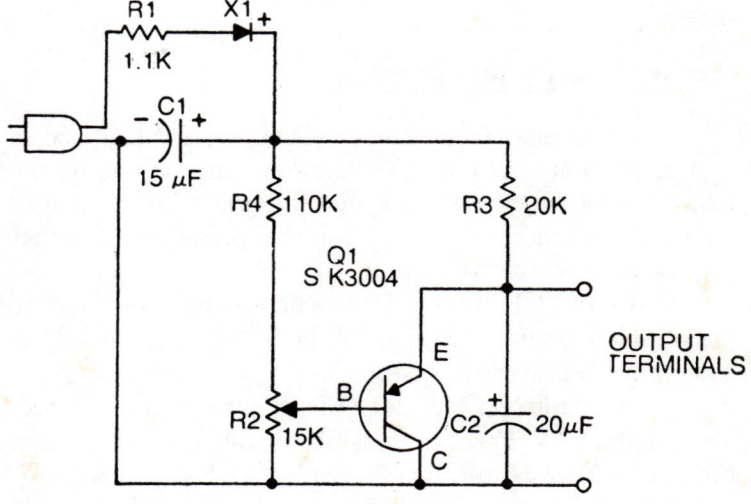

Fig. 6. Transistor power supply circuit.

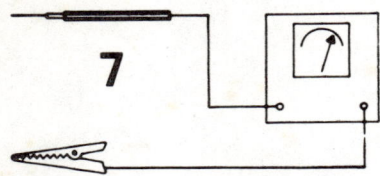

Homemade RF Probe

Your vacuum-tube voltmeter is a very versatile piece of test equipment, but you may lack something if you do not own an rf probe to use with it. This probe allows you to check all points of a circuit for the presence of either wanted or unwanted rf current.

Capacitor C1 blocks direct current but allows rf to pass, which is then rectified by diode X1. Resistor R1 is part of the necessary filter. See Fig. 7 and Table 7.

To use, turn on the piece of equipment to be tested. Turn on the VTVM aset to a positive dc range. Now check at the grid and plate terminals of the unit being tested. Rf should be present and should measure considerably more at the plate terminal than at the grid terminal.

Table 7. Parts List for Homemade RF Probe.

Item No.	Description
C1	.0002-μF, 1000-volt ceramic capacitor.
R1	4.7meg resistor.
X1	1N38B diode.

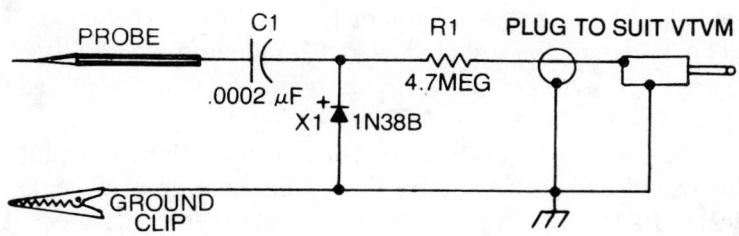

Fig. 7. Rf probe circuit.

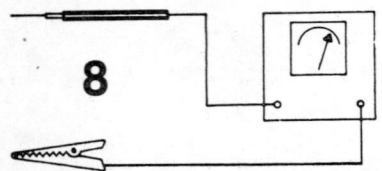

Inexpensive Impedance Checker

An impedance checker is often thought to be beyond the reach of most technicians. If you are willing to invest a few dollars and some of your time, you can put together a serviceable and reasonably accurate one of your own.

A three-gang volume-control type potentiometer is used as the calibrated variable resistance. A single-pole three-position switch is used to select any one of the three ranges. The three-gang potentiometer is not something you will ordinarily find in your spare-parts box; however, the cost is not as much as you would expect. The IRC type PQ11-108 is the basic 1000-ohm potentiometer. IRC type M11-116 is a 10,000-ohm add-on section. IRC M11-128 is a 100,000 ohm add-on section. Assembly is simple, as instructions are finished with the add-on sections. Switch S2 permits switching from one potentiometer to another.

Arrange the components so that the 3-gang control will be at about the center of the enclosure you choose. The two switches should also be mounted on the front panel. Arrange the six terminal points as you prefer. See Fig. 8 and Table 8.

To calibrate, draw three concentric circles on a white card and cement it around the potentiometer shaft. Start calibration with the 1000-ohm potentiometer. Connect a volt-ohmmeter or vacuum-tube voltmeter of known accuracy across it. Start at 1000 ohms and move down to 900 ohms, setting the potentiometer to read exactly 900 ohms. Now draw a line on the card at the point of the control knob. Do the same at 800 ohms. You may wish to place scale marks at 825, 875, etc. When this potentiometer is calibrated, proceed with the 10,000-ohm one, then the 100,000-ohm one.

To use the impedance checker, a component of unknown impedance is connected across the appropriate terminals. A signal generator is connected to the terminals prepared for it. A VTVM is connected across the last two terminals. As switch S1 is switched back and forth you will notice different readings on the VTVM. Adjust the calibrated potentiometer until both readings on the VTVM are the same. Read the impedance of the unknown component on the calibrated dial.

Table 8. Parts List for Impedance Checker.

Item No.	Description

R1,R2,R3	3-gang linear-taper potentiometer composed of the following:
	    1000-ohm potentiometer (IRC type PQ11-108, or equiv.).
	    10,000-ohm potentiometer (IRC type M11-116, or equiv.).
	    100,000-ohm potentiometer (IRC type M11-128, or equiv.).

S1	Spdt switch.
S2	Sp 3-position switch (Oak Series 200 or equiv.).

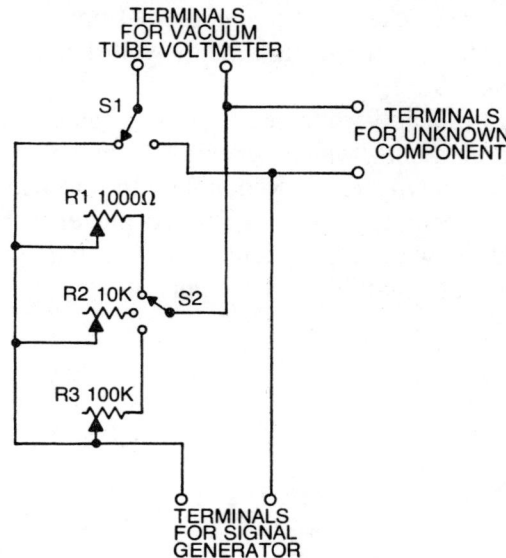

Fig. 8. Impedance checker circuit.

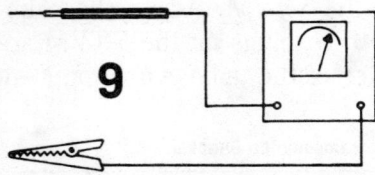

Experimenter's Power Supply

One of the most useful of all items of test equipment is a good power supply built for use on the test bench. The supply shown here will produce the stated voltages without too much variation. This is especially true of the 150-volt B+ section which uses an OA2 gas-filled regulator tube to maintain the voltage at 150 volts. Finally, 6.3 volts are available if needed for filament supply.

There is nothing critical in the circuit. Lay the components on the chassis and plan the set-up before you start cutting. This will result in a neat, well-done job. See Fig. 9 and Table 9.

This is a full-wave rectifier with choke input to the filtering elements which will result in an output of dc without ac components. Remember the ac hum you have heard on some receivers or record players? You can be confident in your experimenting or testing that there is none produced by this power supply.

Table 9. Parts List for Experimenter's Power Supply.

Item No.	Description
C1	20-20 μF, dual-section electrolytic capacitor.
F1	1-A fuse.
L1	6-H, 200-mA filter choke (Allied Radio No. 54B4705 or equiv.).
L2	4.5-H, 200-mA filter choke (Allied Radio No. 54B2347 or equiv.).
R1	3.3k, 25-watt, wirewound resistor.
R2	50k, 10-watt, wirewound resistor.
S1, S2	Spst switches.
T1	Power transformer: primary, 117 Vac; secondary, 350-0-350 Vac at 120 mA, 5 Vac at 3 mA, 6.3 Vac at 4.7 mA center-tapped (Allied Radio No. 54B2044 or equiv.).
V1	5U4G rectifier tube.
V2	OA2 voltage-regulator tube.

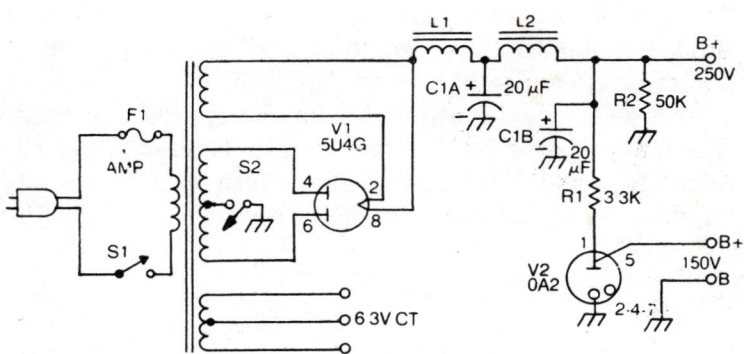

Fig. 9. Experimenter's power supply circuit.

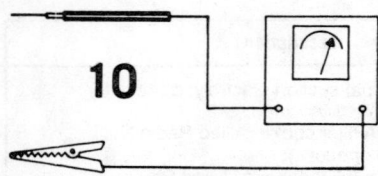

Ham's RF Meter

For a ham or CB operator, an rf meter is a very useful piece of equipment. This inexpensive rf indicator can be used to check transmitter tuning and it can also be used as a field strength meter. You can use it as a transmitter monitor, since any change in indicated signal will mean that a change has taken place in the transmitter, feed line, or antenna.

Construction is simple, but care should be taken to use good construction practices. The meter, S1, S2, C1, and R1, should appear on the front of the box or cabinet that you choose as an enclosure. The antenna can be a short length of wire, the length depending on the power of the transmitter. See Fig. 10 and Table 10.

To use, set the switch S1 for the appropriate band. (For CB use, set S1 as indicated for 10 meters.) Close S2. Adjust R1 to set the meter to zero. Turn on the transmitter and tune C1 for maximum meter reading.

Table 10. Parts List for Ham's RF Meter.

Item No.	Description
C1	140-pF variable capacitor (E. F. Johnson No. 149-6 or equiv.).
C2	.0015-μF capacitor.
L1	No. 24 wire on 1-inch diameter coil form, 32 turns per inch (B&W Miniductor No. 3016 or equiv., 37 turns long).
B1	1.5-V battery.
M1	0—1-mA dc meter (Allied Radio No. 52B7614 or equiv.).
Q1	SK3004 transistor.
R1	10k potentiometer.
R2,R3	620-ohm resistors.
S1	Sp 4-position switch.
S2	Spdt switch.
X1	1N38B diode.

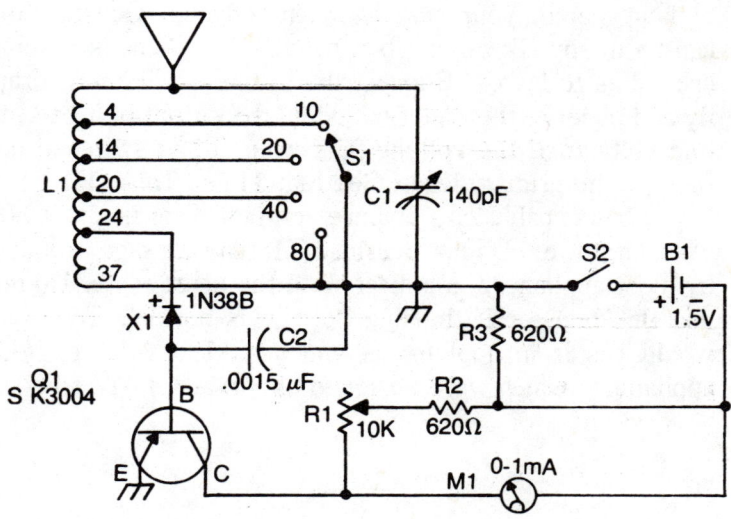

Fig. 10. Rf meter circuit.

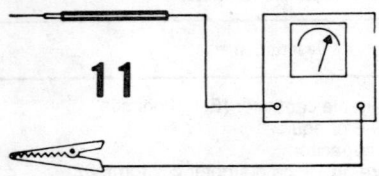

Line-Voltage Booster

Are you in an area where the line voltage varies considerably? Do you have a problem holding the picture in sync on your TV set? This line voltage booster is just the thing for you if your problem is one of low voltage. This unit can also be used by hams who must operate from a portable source on field day. Low voltage from gasoline-powered generators can cause plenty of problems.

The two most expensive parts of the booster are the meter and the filament transformer. If you have one or both available, your cost is much reduced. Construction can be in any convenient box or chassis. There is nothing critical as to layout. Connect the primary of T1 temporarily and observe the effect of adding the output of T1 to the line voltage. If the voltage falls when T1 is switched on, reverse the primary leads. See Fig. 11 and Table 11.

T1 is capable of 3 amperes output. This is about 300 watts of power. Do not overload T1. The wattage required by most appliances is indicated on the name plate. Do not use this booster if the line voltage is normal. To do so would result in applying as much as 130 volts to your appliances, which were designed to operate at 117 volts.

Table 11. Parts List for Line-Voltage Booster.

Item No.	Description
M1	0-150 Vac meter (Allied Radio No. 52B7666 or equiv.).
M2,M3	Chassis-type receptacles.
S1	Dpdt switch.
S2	Spdt switch.
T1	12-volt filament transformer, center-tapped (Allied Radio No. 54B4709 or equiv.).

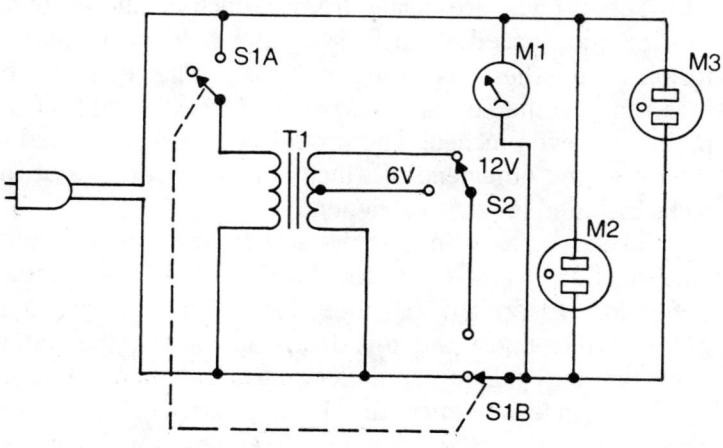

Fig. 11. Line-voltage booster circuit.

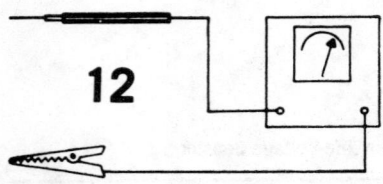

Transistorized Moisturemeter

How can you tell when your lawn needs water—when the grass begins to yellow? By then it is too late; some damage has already been done and if you water more frequently, the water bill becomes larger each time. What is the answer? Build this interesting little moisturemeter.

The circuit is simple and works like this: A small current passes between the probes and is amplified by the transistor to deflect the meter.

The probes are made from ⅛-inch diameter brass brazing rod spaced ½ inch apart and held in a block of formica or other insulating material. The ends to be inserted into the soil are sharpened. Overall length of the probes is seven inches. The probes are each connected to a wire on the other end of which is a phone tip to suit the jacks installed in your instrument.

R1 serves as a limiting resistor to limit the maximum current flow to a value that will provide total meter deflection. Insert a 750k potentiometer in the circuit in place of R1. Short the test leads and adjust the potentiometer until full meter deflection is obtained. Measure the resistance at which the 750k potentiometer is set. This is the value of R1. Solder a fixed resistor of approximately that value into the circuit. See Fig. 12 and Table 12.

In use, a half-scale deflection indicates adequate moisture. Below that amount, watering may be needed. Best results are obtained when you become familiar with the use of the meter, as each soil will have a different value of resistance because of its pH.

Table 12. Parts List for Transistorized Moisturemeter.

Item No.	Description
B1	15-volt battery.
M2,M3	Miniature phone jacks.
M1	0-5 milliammeter (Allied Radio No. 52B8970 or equiv.).
Q1	2N228 transistor.
R1	510k resistor (see test).
S1	Spst switch.

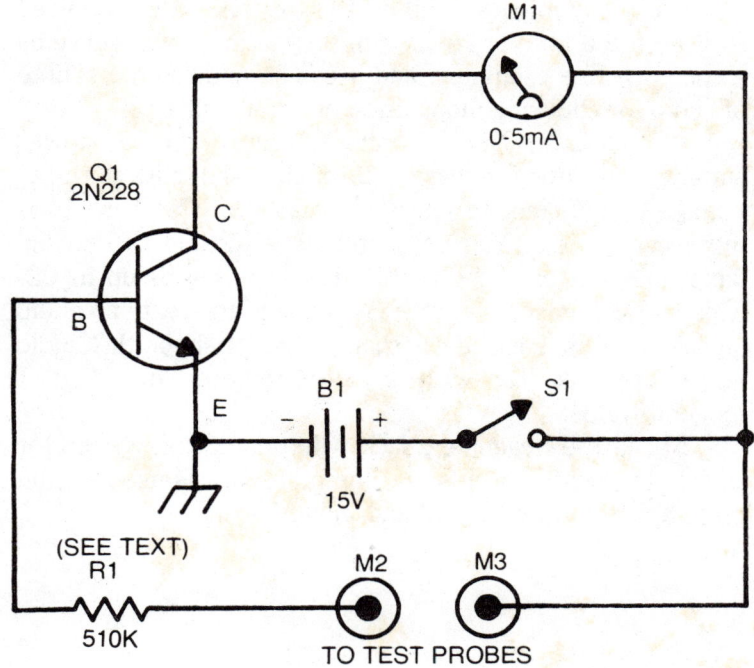

Fig. 12. Moisturemeter circuit.

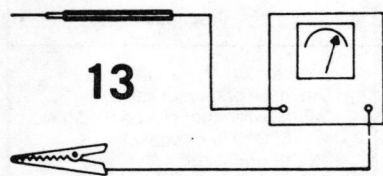

Neon-Lamp Tone Generator

A neon-lamp tone generator has several uses, any one of which will pay for the small cost of this one. It can be used to generate a tone to check a hi-fi system, it will serve as a code practice oscillator, and it can be used as the source of audio for checking modulation of a transmitter.

In this unit, X1, R1, and C1 make up the power supply. Capacitor C2 charges through resistor R2 until the voltage is sufficient to light the lamp M3. This lamp uses more current than can be supplied by R2 and C2, so the lamp goes out until the required voltage builds up in C2. This all takes place at a rate fast enough to create an audio signal. If it is desired to change the pitch of the audio signal, replace R2 with a potentiometer of about 1 megohm value.

M2 is the headphone jack when using this generator as a code-practice oscillator. The other jack is used for the telegraph key. See Fig. 13 and Table 13.

Table 13. Parts List for Neon-Lamp Tone Generator.

Item No.	Description
C1	30-μF, 250-volt electrolytic capacitor.
C2	.003-μF capacitor.
M1	Open-circuit phone jack.
M2	Normally-closed phone jack.
M3	NE-2E neon lamp.
R1	51k resistor.
R2	510k resistor.
T1	Transformer (Utah Type 1755 or equiv.).
X1	Rectifier (GE-504A or equiv.).

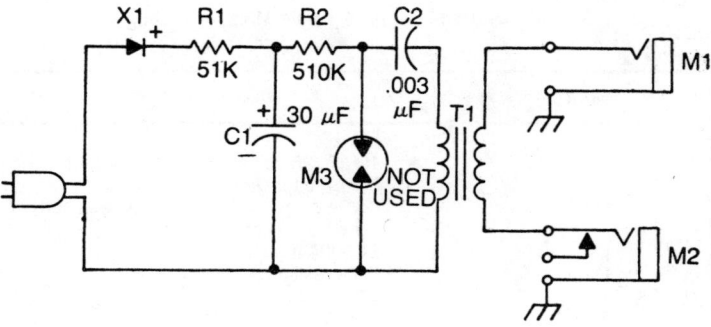

Fig. 13. Tone generator circuit.

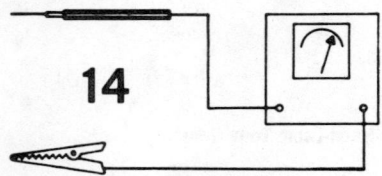

14

Dynamic Mike For Testing

Have you priced microphones lately, especially some of the better ones? Here is a reason for making your own.

This unit can be built in any small plastic box. The speaker is taken from a defunct transistor radio and takes the place of the mike cartridge. The impedance of most speakers is quite low; however, coupled with the SK3004 transistor indicated here, the impedance is raised to a point where it is comparable to commercial dynamic microphones. See Fig. 14 and Table 14.

Table 14. Parts List for Dynamic Mike for Testing.

Item No.	Description
C1	15-μF, 25-volt electrolytic capacitor.
C2	0.5-μF capacitor.
B1	(2) 9-volt transistor radio batteries connected in series.
Q1	SK3004 transistor.
R1	510k resistor.
R2	24k resistor.
S1	Spst switch.
SP1	Speaker, miniature or subminiature, 8- or 10-ohm voice coil.

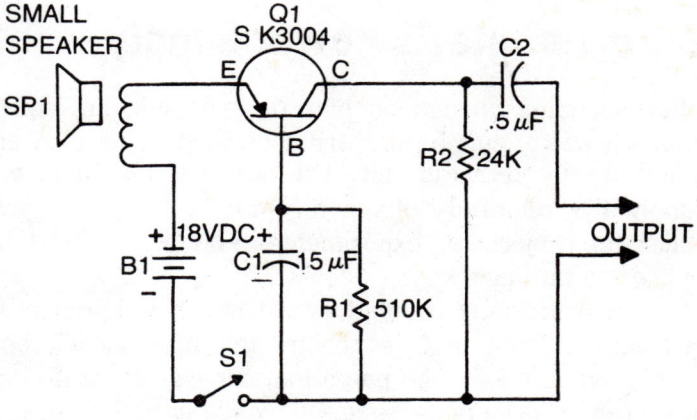

Fig. 14. Dynamic mike circuit.

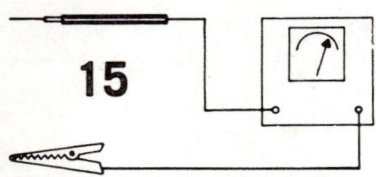

15

Transistor Experimenter's Power Supply

After spending enough on batteries to build an experimenter's power supply, the writer decided to get busy and build a really versatile unit. The one described here will supply the required voltage for practically any of your transistor projects or experiments. Voltage is controlled by merely turning a knob.

Construction is straightforward and should present no problems. If the unit is constructed in a closed box, provide ventilation. The potentiometer will generate heat as there is considerable current flowing through it.

In use, connect the supply to your experiment after setting the "no load" voltage to the desired figure. If an exact voltage is desired, it may be necessary to reset the control after placing a load on the power supply. See Fig. 15 and Table 15.

Table 15. Parts List for Transistor Experimenter's Power Supply.

Item No.	Description
C1	20-20 µF dual-section, 150-volt electrolytic capacitor (Allied Radio No. 43B9252 or equiv.).
M1	0-30 Vdc meter (Allied Radio No. 52B8980 or equiv.).
R1	500-ohm, 25-watt wirewound potentiometer.
R2	100-ohm, 25-watt resistor.
R3	15k, 10-watt resistor.
S1	Spst switch.
T1	25-volt filament transformer (Allied Radio No. 54B1421 or equiv.).
X1	Rectifier (GE-504A or equiv.).

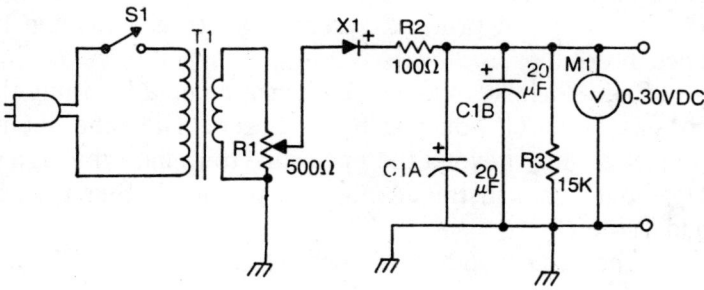

Fig. 15. Experimenter's power supply circuit.

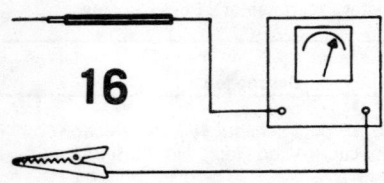

One-Tube Frequency Standard

Do you want a good 500kHz frequency standard to use with your ham receiver? If so, here is one that is not expensive to build.

No power supply is required since power is taken from your receiver. Careful construction to obtain maximum rigidity of the frequency-controlling elements is important since the slightest movement of components or connecting leads will result in some frequency change. However, if you proceed carefully no trouble should be encountered.

The rf choke should be firmly mounted within the chassis or metal box you have chosen. The tube should project slightly beyond the enclosure to radiate the signal. Openings for adjustment must be provided. See Fig. 16 and Table 16.

When the standard is completed, tune to WWV and calibrate.

Table 16. Parts List for One-Tube Frequency Standard.

Item No.	Description
C1	.0047-µF disc ceramic capacitor.
C2	270-pF disc ceramic capacitor.
C3	60-pF miniature trimmer (Allied Radio No. 43B7090 or equiv.).
C4	7-pF miniature trimmer (Allied Radio No. 43B7087 or equiv.).
L1	2.5-mH rf choke (National R-100 or equiv. tapped between first and second pies from ground end).
R1	47k resistor.
S1	Spst switch.
V1	6100 tube.

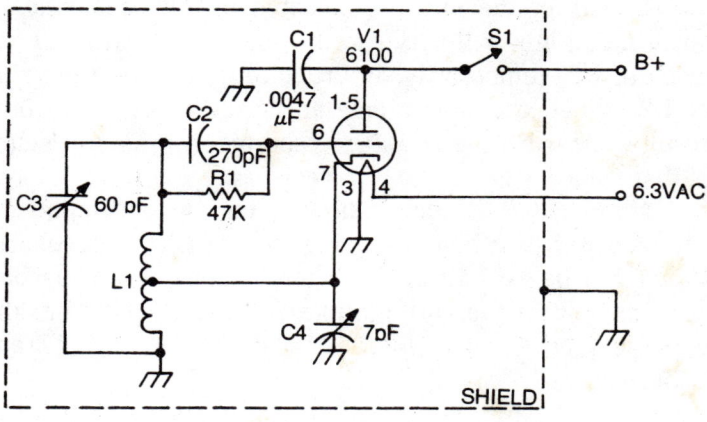

Fig. 16. Frequency standard circuit.

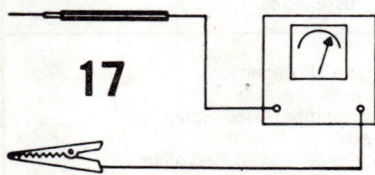

Crystal Microphone Substitute

There are many carbon microphones that are available for the asking, simply because very few items of equipment now use carbon microphones. For a small expenditure and a little work, you can make any good carbon mike work into a crystal mike input.

Construct the unit as indicated in the schematic. A small metal box will serve well. Insert a potentiometer in place of R2, temporarily, in order to determine the value of R2. When the potentiometer is set to give the best results, measure the resistance and insert a fixed resistor of that value.

Note that it is important that microphone inputs be shielded well. Without shielding, the penalty is feedback, which can be so bad that the microphone is not usable. The input from the carbon mike and the output from the unit must be shielded for best results. See Fig. 17 and Table 17.

Table 17. Parts List for Crystal Microphone Substitute.

Item No.	Description
C1	.01-μF capacitor.
B1	3-volt battery.
R1	100-ohm resistor.
R2	See text.
S1	Spst switch.

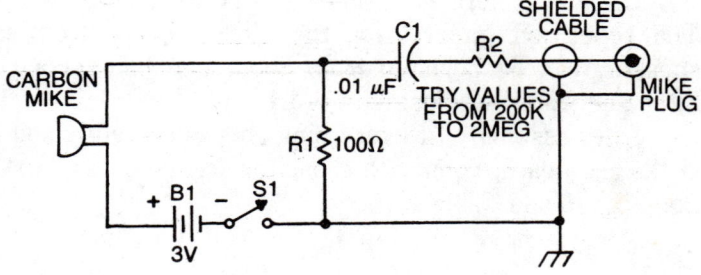

Fig. 17. Microphone circuit.

39

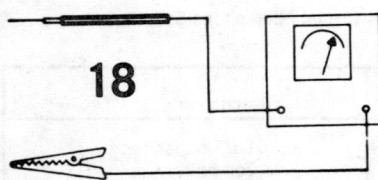

Electronic Timer

This is a very simple electronic timer which will have many obvious uses. It can, for instance, be used in a dark room. It can be used anywhere that it is convenient to time an operation by counting audible clicks at predetermined intervals.

L1 shown here is a Meissner 14-1071 antenna coil. The repetition interval for the clicks, heard from the speaker, can be adjusted from about one half-second to fifteen seconds by adjustment of L1.

After assembly, if everything checks correctly and no clicks are heard, connect a capacitor across L1 as shown. See Fig. 18 and Table 18.

Table 18. Parts List for Electronic Timer.

Item No.	Description
C1	100-μF 15-volt electrolytic capacitor.
C2	See text.
L1	Antenna coil (Meissner 14-1071 or equiv.).
B1	6-volt battery
Q1	2N525 transistor.
S1	Spst switch.
SP1	Speaker, 3.2 to not more than 16 ohms voice-coil impedance.
X1	1N34 diode.

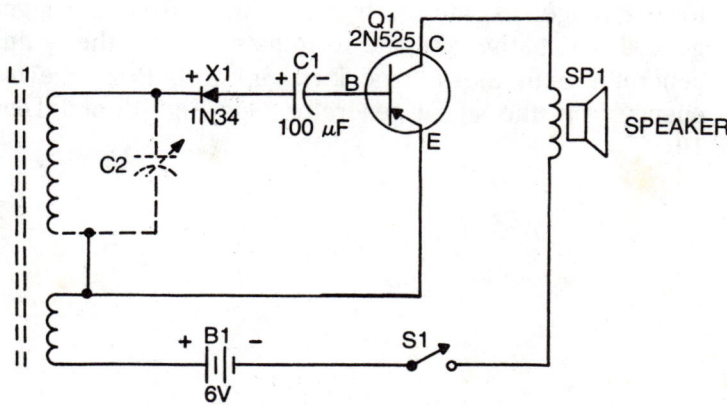

Fig. 18. Electronic timer circuit.

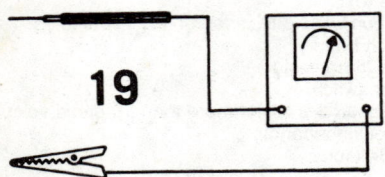

Intermediate-Frequency Checker

Those i-f transformers that are taking up space in the shop could be put to use, but how can they be used if the frequency is not known? Here is how you may answer that question at minimum cost.

Connect a 20,000 ohms-per-volt voltmeter, set at the lowest range, as shown. Inject a signal from the signal generator at the proper terminals. Tune the signal generator until the voltage kicks upward. Read the frequency from the signal generator. See Fig. 19 and Table 19.

Table 19. Parts List for Intermediate-Frequency Checker.

Item No	Description
C1	10-pF capacitor.
L1	2.4-μH choke (J.W. Miller 4606 or equiv.).
X1	1N38B diode.

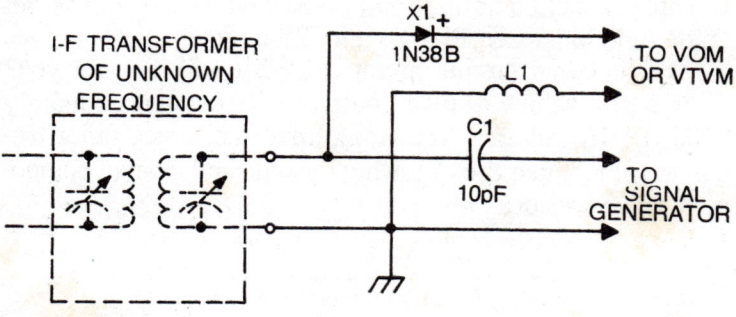

Fig. 19. Intermediate-frequency checker circuit.

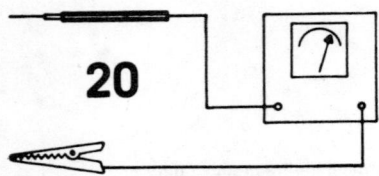

20

Simple Astable Multivibrator

You have read about astable multivibrators but probably figured they were more theory than anything else. Here is one you can build and put to immediate use around the workbench.

Free-running, or astable, multivibrators develop square-wave outputs generally equal to their dc supply voltage on output peaks; minimum values are closer to the collector saturation voltage of the transistors employed. The circuit shown in the accompanying diagram is no exception. Here, the unit is a two-stage oscillator that operates as follows: One stage conducts at saturation while the other is cut off until a point is reached where both stages trade functions. See Fig. 20 and Table 20.

So much for circuit operation. What will it do for you? With parts values shown, output will be approximately 7000 Hz. However, if you would like to produce other frequencies, just use the following formula and change component values accordingly:

$$f = \frac{1}{(0.7\ C1R2) + (0.7\ C2R3)}$$

Table 20. Parts List for Simple Astable Multivibrator.

Item No.	Description
C1,C2	.1-μF capacitor.
B1	12-volt battery.
Q1,Q2	2N1481 transistors.
R1,R4	62-ohm, 5-watt resistors.
R2,R3	1K,5-watt resistors.
S1	Spst switch.

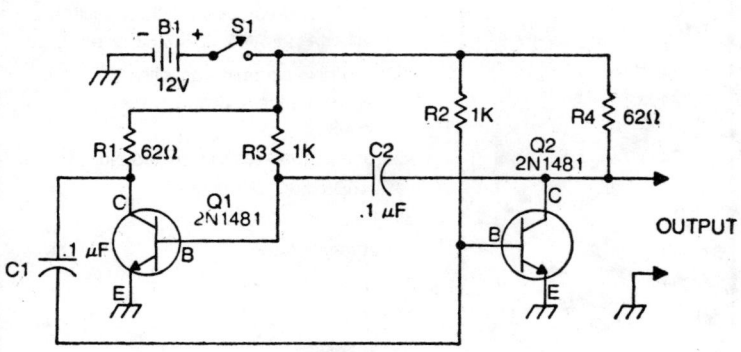

Fig. 20. Astable multivibrator circuit.

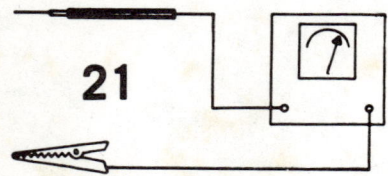

Ham's Audio Oscillator

This is a useful CW oscillator for the radio ham. It also provides an opportunity to use a rather unusual tube, the 117P7 shown in the schematic.

You will note that there is no power supply as we know it for the circuit. The diode section of the 117P7 rectifies the 117 Vac to provide B+ for the second half.

Note that this circuit is grounded at only one place, at the speaker. See Fig. 21 and Table 21.

Table 21. Parts List for Ham's Audio Oscillator.

Item No.	Description
C1	20-20 μF, 250-volt electrolytic capacitor. (Allied Radio No. 43B9263 or equiv.).
C2,C3	.025-μF disc ceramic capacitor.
M1,M2	Closed circuit jacks (Allied No. 47B4963 or equiv.).
R1	250-ohm, 5-watt resistor (Allied No. 45B5250C or equiv.).
R2	3k, 1-watt resistor.
R3	15k potentiometer.
R4	350-ohm potentiometer.
S1	Spst switch.
SP1	PM speaker.
T1	Universal output transformer (Allied No. 54B2023 or equiv.).
V1	117P7 tube.

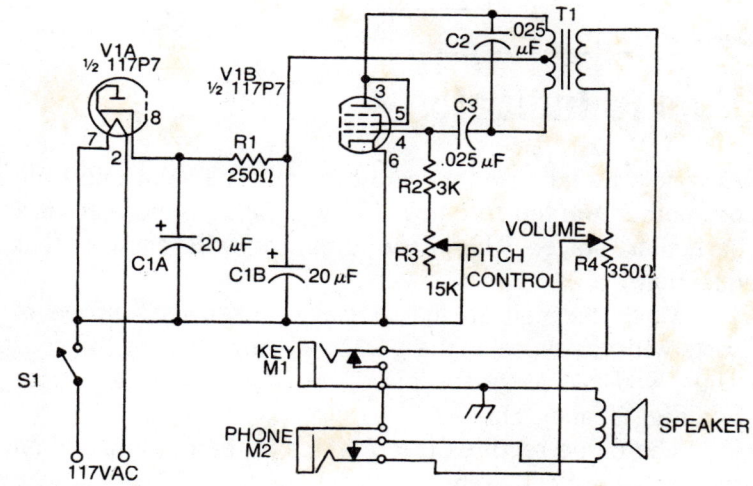

Fig. 21. Audio oscillator circuit.

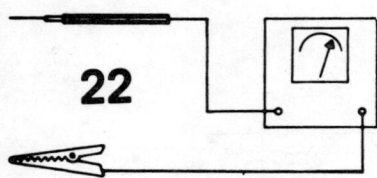

Vom Rf Indicator

Anyone who has used a radio transmitter has at one time or another wanted to know if rf was being generated at a particular stage. This little gimmick will answer that question.

Make the coil so that it can be used as a probe of sorts with the diode at the VOM and long leads to the coil. Thus, you can move the pickup coil from stage to stage. See Fig. 22 and Table 22.

The diode rectifies the rf which is then read as dc on the lowest voltage scale.

Table 22. Parts List for VOM RF Indicator.

Item No.	Description
L1	6 turns insulated wire, closewound in a ¾-inch diameter coil.
X1	1N38B.

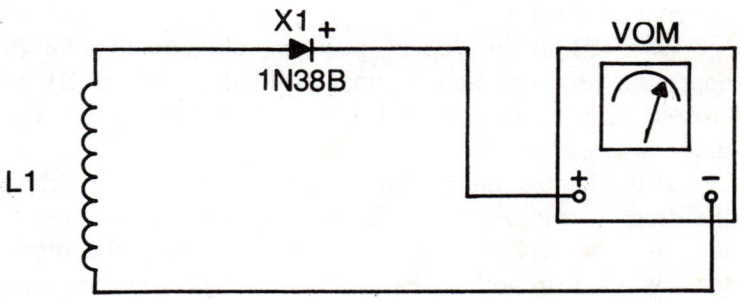

Fig. 22. Rf indicator circuit.

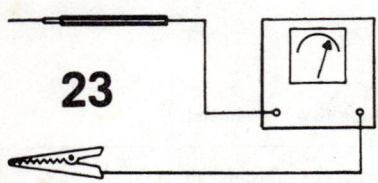

High-Voltage Silicon Rectifier Checker

Need a quick way to test those 120-volt silicon rectifier diodes around the workbench?

The circuit shown in the accompanying diagram provides a simple "good/bad" test circuit. Just plug the rectifier in question into the circuit in place of X1 and you are ready to test.

With S1 in the "open" position, M1 should light to approximately one-half normal brilliance. When S1 is closed, the lamp should brighten considerably—if the diode is any good.

If the lamp comes to full brilliance with S1 open, then the diode is shorted. If the lamp is on when S1 is closed, but goes out completely when S1 is opened, the diode itself is open. In both cases, chalk up a "bad" rectifier. See Fig. 23 and Table 23.

Table 23. Parts List for High Voltage Silicon Rectifier Checker.

Item No.	Description
M1	25-watt household light bulb.
S1	Spst switch.
X1	HV silicon rectifier under test (see text).

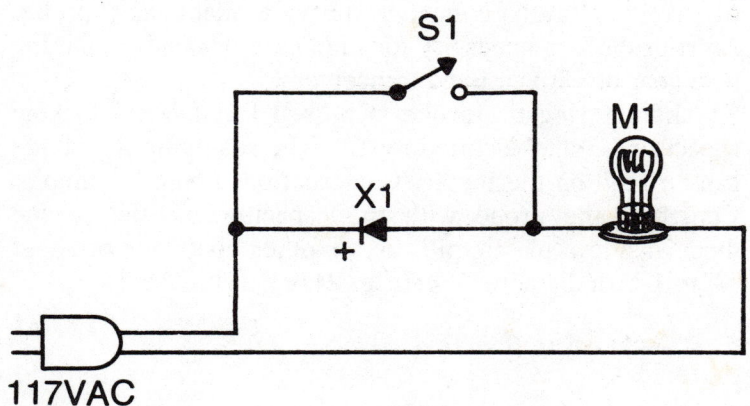

Fig. 23. High-voltage silicon rectifier checker circuit.

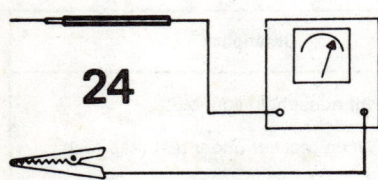

Diode Rf Probe

Practically everyone has a VOM or a VTVM, but not everyone is fortunate enough to have available an rf probe. An rf probe is a necessity for tuning up or troubleshooting ham gear or Citizen Band tranceivers.

Rf entering the probe is passed through dc-blocking capacitor C1 and rectified by X1. The resultant dc voltage can be read on the meter. Construction should be simple. Construct the probe with the capacitors, resistor, and diode inside a plastic pill box or other container of about ¾- to 1-inch diameter. See Fig. 24 and Table 24.

Table 24. Parts List for Diode RF Probe.

Item No.	Description
C1	100-pF capacitor.
C2	.015-μF capacitor.
R1	2.2meg resistor.
X1	1N38B diode.

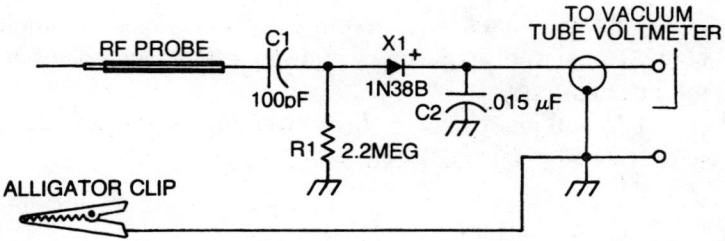

Fig. 24. Rf probe circuit.

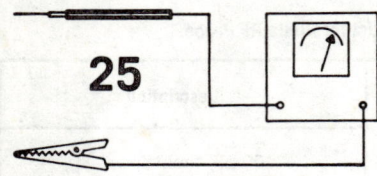

One-Transistor CB Field Strength Meter

Every CB'er needs a good field strength meter. A field strength meter is useful when tuning the transmitter, adjusting the antenna, and monitoring the operation of your rig.

This one uses an inexpensive meter and a single-stage transistor amplifier which in effect increases the meter sensitivity.

The antenna can be a three- to four-foot length of stiff wire. See Fig. 25 and Table 25.

Table 25. Parts List for CB Field Strength Meter.

Item No.	Description
C1	3—32-pF (E.F. Johnson 160-130 or equiv. miniature variable).
C2	.001-μF capacitor.
L1	12 turns, No. 14 wire ⅝-inch diameter, 1 inch long—equally spaced.
B1	4.5-volt battery.
M1	0-1, 0-2, or 0-5 mA meter.
Q1	SK3004 transistor.
R1	20k potentiometer (Allied No. 30U309 or equiv.).
S1	Spst switch.
X1	1N38B diode.

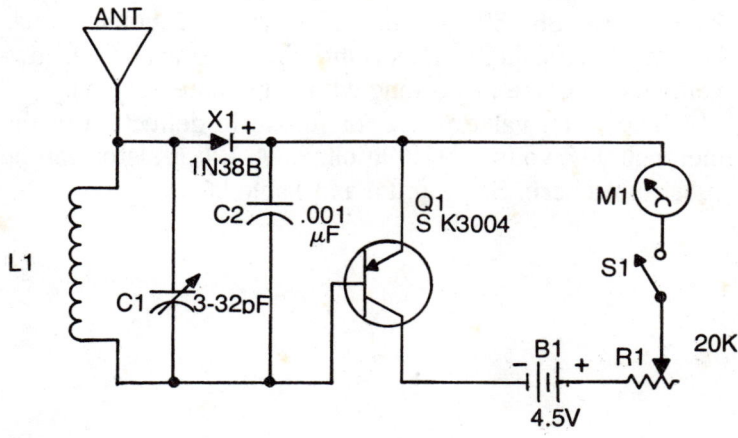

Fig. 25. Field strength meter circuit.

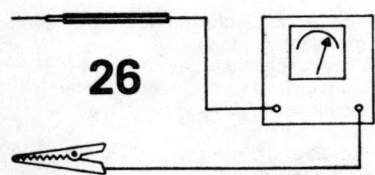

Dial-A-Volt Miniature Power Supply

This is one of the most useful pieces of equipment for the home shop. This power supply will provide voltages of 1.1, 1.4, 1.5, 2.0, 2.5, 3.0, 3.3, 4.0, 5.0, 6.3, 7.0, 7.5, 12, 20, 25, 30, 35, 50, 70, 85, 110, and 117 volts. It has become increasingly important to have available low-voltage dc for use in working with solid state devices.

The exact value of R1 for full-scale deflection of the meter at 117 volts is 11,690 ohms. A 12k resistor can be substituted here. See Fig. 26 and Table 26.

Table 26. Parts List for Dial-A-Volt Miniature Power Supply.

Item No.	Description
C1	40-40 µF, 250-volt, dual-section electrolytic capacitor (Cornell-Dubilier Type 40-250 or equiv.).
L1	Choke (Allied Radio No. 54B2345 or equiv.).
M1	0-1 milliammeter (see test).
M2	Jack (Allied Radio No. 47C1328 or equiv.).
R1	12k resistor.
S1	Spst switch.
S2	24-point tap switch (Mallory No. 13124L or equiv.).
T1	Tube-tester transformer (Allied Radio No. 54B2083 or equiv.).
X1	1N158 diode.

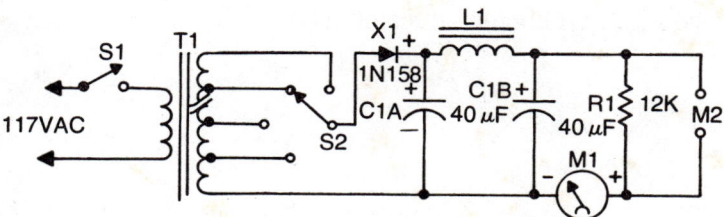

Fig. 26. Miniature power supply circuit.

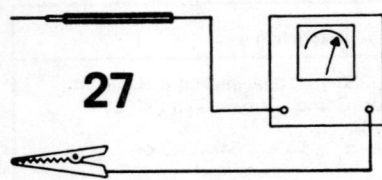

Two-Transistor Sine-Wave Generator

A sine-wave generator may be used for distortion tests, for testing gain of electronic stages, and as a signal generator to locate defective components. Since this unit has no very large components, it may be constructed in a small metal box.

L1 is a small choke. Ours was a small output transformer. Use the high impedance winding if you wish to do likewise. See Fig. 27 and Table 27

The frequency of the sine wave may be decreased by increasing the values of C1 and C2. The ratio of capacitance C1 to C2 should be maintained.

Table 27. Parts List for Two-Transistor Sine-Wave Generator.

Item No.	Description
C1	.01-µF capacitor.
C2	.1-µF capacitor.
C3	.3-µF capacitor.
C4	.2-µF capacitor.
L1	Small choke about 14,000 ohms impedance (See text).
B1	15-volt battery.
Q1,Q2	SK3004 transistors.
R1	18k resistor.
R2	12k resistor.
R3	1.1k resistor.
R4	75k resistor.
R5	7.5k potentiometer.
S1	Spst switch.

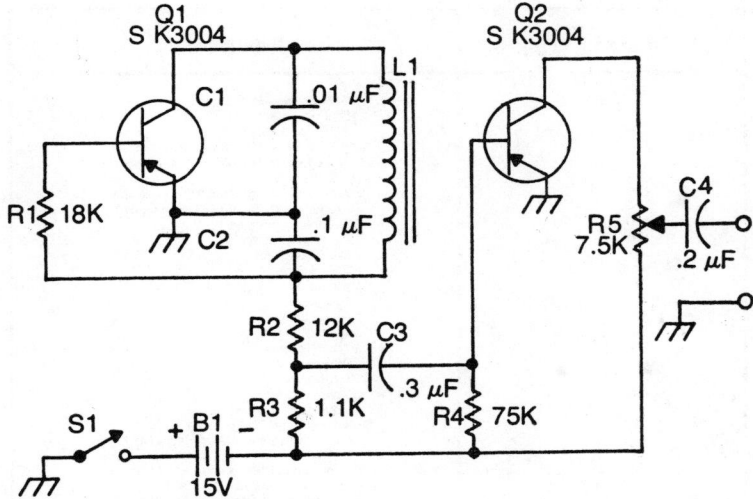

Fig. 27. Sine-wave generator circuit.

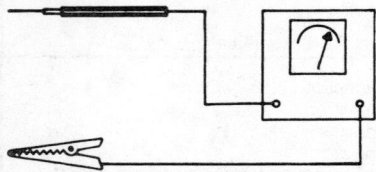

Sound Level Meter

A sound level meter is perhaps not needed as often as the more basic items of test equipment. You may wish to use one when checking out performance of PA systems or relative noise level in an industrial plant.

This is basically an audio amplifier circuit and as such you should experience no difficulty with construction. Keep leads short and keep input and output leads of each stage as far apart as possible to avoid oscillation. See Fig. 28 and Table 28.

Table 28. Parts List for Sound Level Meter.

Item No.	Description
C1	0047-µF capacitor.
C2	15-µF capacitor.
C3,C5	01-µF capacitors.
C4	10-µF, 50-volt, electrolytic capacitor. (Allied Radio No. 43B9223 or equiv.).
C6	.1-µF capacitor.
C7	30-30 µF, 250-volt electrolytic capacitor. (Allied Radio No. 43B9296 or equiv.).
M1	0-500 microammeter.
R1	150k potentiometer
R2	11meg resistor.
R3,R4	270k resistors.
R5	1meg resistor
R6	30k resistor.
R7	51k resistor.
R8	240-ohm, 2-watt resistor
R9	1.1meg resistor.
R10	12k resistor.
R11	1k, 5-watt resistor
R12	56-ohm resistor.
S1	Spst switch
SP1	4-inch or larger PM speaker
T1	Output transformer (Allied Radio No. 54B2023 or equiv)
T2	Power transformer primary, 117 Vac, secondary, 125 Vac 15 mA, 6.3 Vac .6 A (Allied Radio No 54B1410 or equiv)
V1	6BA6 tube
V2	6060 tube
X1	1N38B diode
X2	SK3016 diode

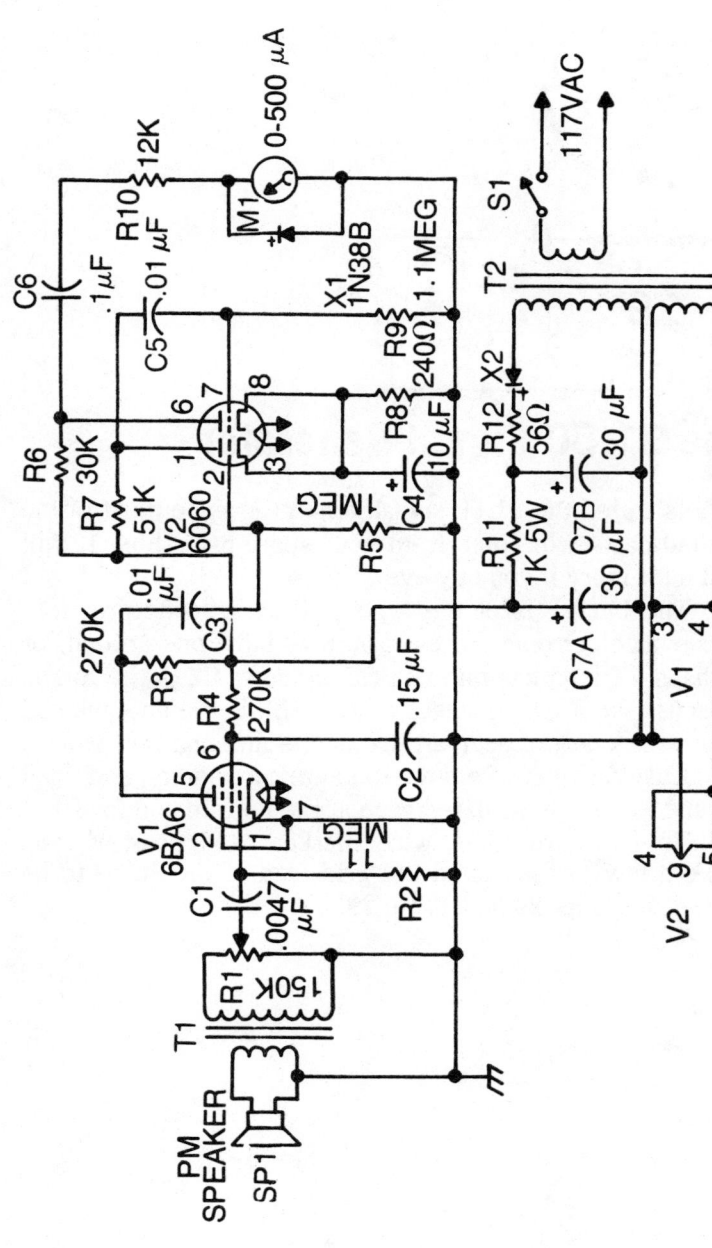

Fig. 28. Sound level meter circuit.

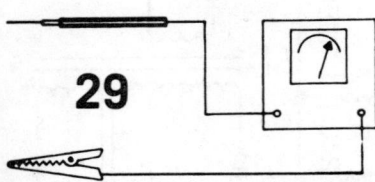

29

The $1.50 Signal Generator

This is called the $1.50 signal generator since most of the needed parts will come from your spare-parts box. It will cost a bit more if you buy everything.

The buzzer is of the type sold as a "code practice" buzzer at electronic stores. You may have one around, or perhaps a friend has one you can borrow. C2 is the tuning capacitor from a broadcast receiver. L2 is the antenna coil from a broadcast receiver. L2 is the antenna coil from a broadcast receiver. Remove the antenna winding and wind about 15 turns of insulated wire at the bottom end for L1.

To use, bring the wire marked "to receiver" and make a few turns around the grid lead of the stage to be tested. See Fig. 29 and Table 29.

Table 29. Parts List for The $1.50 Signal Generator.

Item No.	Description
C1	.2-μF capacitor.
C2	365-pF variable capacitor (from discarded broadcast receiver).
L1	See text.
L2	Miller 70-A or equivalent, or antenna coil from discarded broadcast receiver.
B1	Battery to supply correct voltage for buzzer.
M1	Buzzer (see text).
S1	Spst switch.

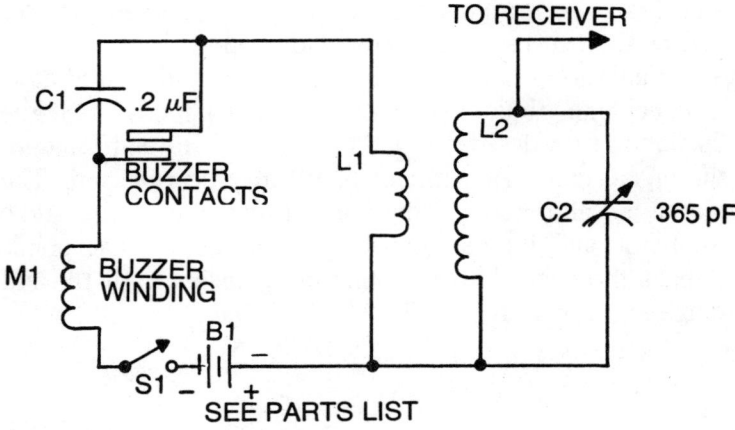

Fig. 29. Signal generator circuit.

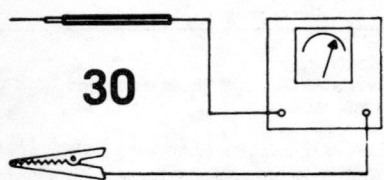

Audio Frequency Meter

An audio frequency meter is used to measure, as the name implies, those frequencies that can be heard. It may be used to measure the tonal range of a beat frequency oscillator, an audio oscillator, or an electronic musical instrument.

This device is a bridge circuit and is used in the following manner: An audio signal is connected to M1. The main tuning control, (R4, R5) is tuned until the audio signal is nulled or almost disappears. The frequency meter setting then corresponds to the audio input.

Calibration should be by use of an audio oscillator. Connect the audio oscillator and headphones. Set the oscillator to a desired frequency. Adjust R5 and R4 until the signal nulls. Adjustment of R2 may be required. The meter is calibrated for the same frequency as the audio oscillator and its dial should be marked at that point. Repeat the procedure for other frequencies until the full range is calibrated. See Fig. 30 and Table 30.

Table 30. Parts List for Audio Frequency Meter.

Item No.	Description
C1, C2	.001-μF capacitors.
M1, M2	Jacks (H. H. Smith Type 224 or equiv.).
R1	1k resistor.
R2	750-phm potentiometer.
R3	2k resistor.
R4, R5	Dual 500k potentiometer.

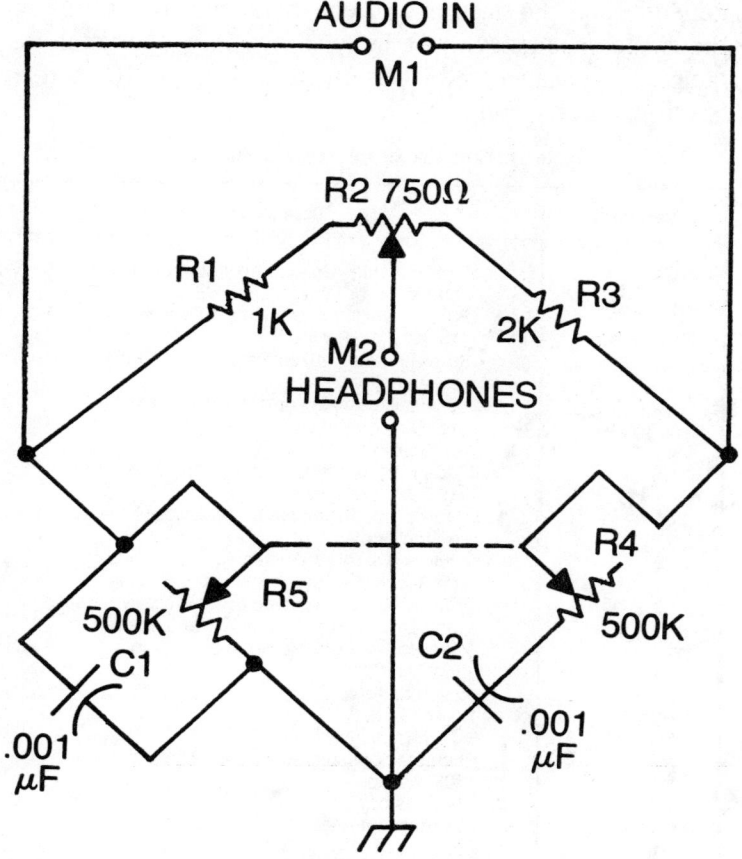

Fig. 30. Audio frequency meter circuit.

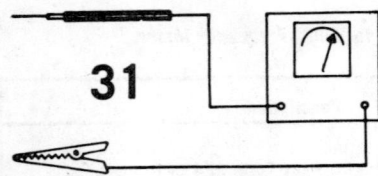

Frequency Meter/Monitor

With this device you have a combination code monitor for your ham rig and a frequency meter. The basic range of this meter is 1685 to 2110 kHz. The exact range will depend upon the accuracy of construction. By multiplying the basic frequency, just as you multiply a crystal frequency, you can extend the range to include 10 meters. See Fig. 31 and Table 31.

Table 31. Parts List for Frequency Meter/Monitor.

Item No.	Description
C1	50-pF variable capacitor (Hammerlund No. MAPC-50 or equiv.).
C2	120-pF silver mica capacitor (Elmenco No. 15-121J or equiv.).
C3	180-pF trimmer (Allied Radio No. 43B3513 or equiv.).
C4	270-pF silver mica capacitor (Elmenco No. 15-271J or equiv.).
C5	.1-µF capacitor.
C6, C7	2000-pF silver mica capacitor (Elmenco No. 19-202J or equiv.).
L1	26 turns No. 26 enameled wire close wound on top of L2.
L2	60 turns No. 26 enameled wire close wound on 6-inch diameter coil form.
L3	24 turns No. 26 enameled wire close wound on same ¾-inch form as L2 and spaced ⅛ inch from ground end.
L4	2.5mH choke.
B1	45 volt battery.
B2	1.5 volt battery.
M1	RCA phono jack.
M2	Phone jack (insulated from chassis).
R1	110k resistor.
R2	47k resistor.
R3	50k potentiometer.
S1	Spst switch.
V1	5910 tube.
V2	1DN5 tube.

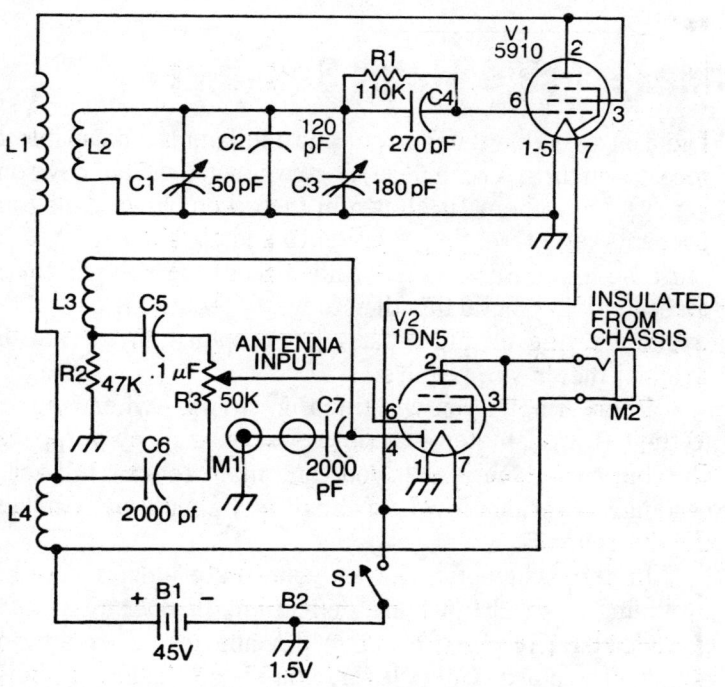

Fig. 31. Frequency meter/monitor circuit.

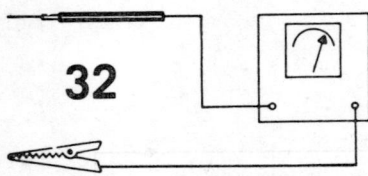

Inexpensive Meter Sensitizer

Did you ever have need for a dc milliammeter capable of measuring the microampere range when you did not have one handy? The schematic shown in the accompanying diagram presents an interesting solution to adding sensitivity to, in our case, 0-1 milliammeter. And chances are you will find it an easier job to build this than to waste the better part of the evening trying to find a parts store open that carries the original meter you require.

Interestingly, you will find this circuit—when coupled to the 0-1 milliameter—capable of serving many purposes. One big advantage is that you can obtain several full-scale readings at various levels of sensitivity simply by readjusting the controls.

In the schematic, R2 is your meter-adjust control, providing desired full-scale deflection. In operation, simply adjust R1 for zero Ico, trin R2, and you are ready for action. If you are really clever, you should be able to build the whole affair behind the meter itself, using hearing-aid type cells for M2 and M3. See Fig. 32 and Table 32.

Table 32. Parts List for Inexpensive Meter Sensitizer.

Item No.	Description
M1	0-1 dc milliammeter.
B1, B2	3-volt batteries.
Q1	HEP-3 transistor.
R1	15k potentiometer.
R2	750-phm potentiometer.
R3	220-ohm resistor.

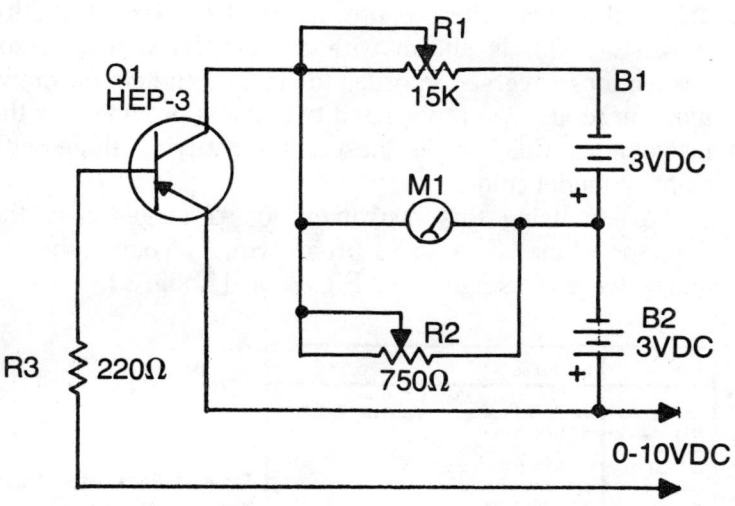

Fig. 32. Meter Sensitizer Circuit.

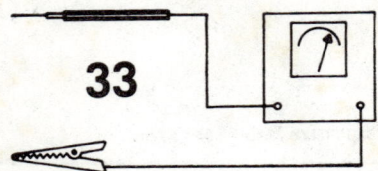

Deluxe Transistor Signal Tracer

This deluxe transistor signal tracer, as the name indicates, is just about the best instrument you can make for this purpose. It uses batteries, consequently there is no possibility of ac hum from the power supply. This unit will provide all of the necessary features of expensive equipment. This tracer can provide almost a watt of rf output.

Plan the parts placement carefully. The circuit is not critical; however, a study of the circuit and careful planning will pay off. Please note that in the circuit, the third transistor, Q3, is shown with the emitter and collector connections reversed in order to simplify the circuit drawing. There are two probes and two inputs provided for the instrument. Color code these by identifying them with paint or model color.

When using this instrument on rf stages, use the detector probe. The audio probe will, of course, be required for audio stages. See Fig. 33 and Table 33.

Item No.	Description
C1, C2, C3	10-μF, 25-volt electrolytic capacitors.
B1	6-volt battery.
M1, M2	RCA phono jacks.
Q1, Q2, Q3	SK3004 transistors.
Q4	SK3009 transistor.
R1, R3	110k resistors.
R2	11k resistor.
R4	25k potentiometer with switch.
R5	51k resistor.
R6	18k resistor.
R7	200k resistor.
R8	300-ohm resistor.
S1	Spst switch (Part of R4).
SP1	Speaker (Utah Replacement Speaker SP57D-M1 or equivalent, connected for 40 ohms impedance).

Table 33. Parts List for Deluxe Transistor Signal Tracer.

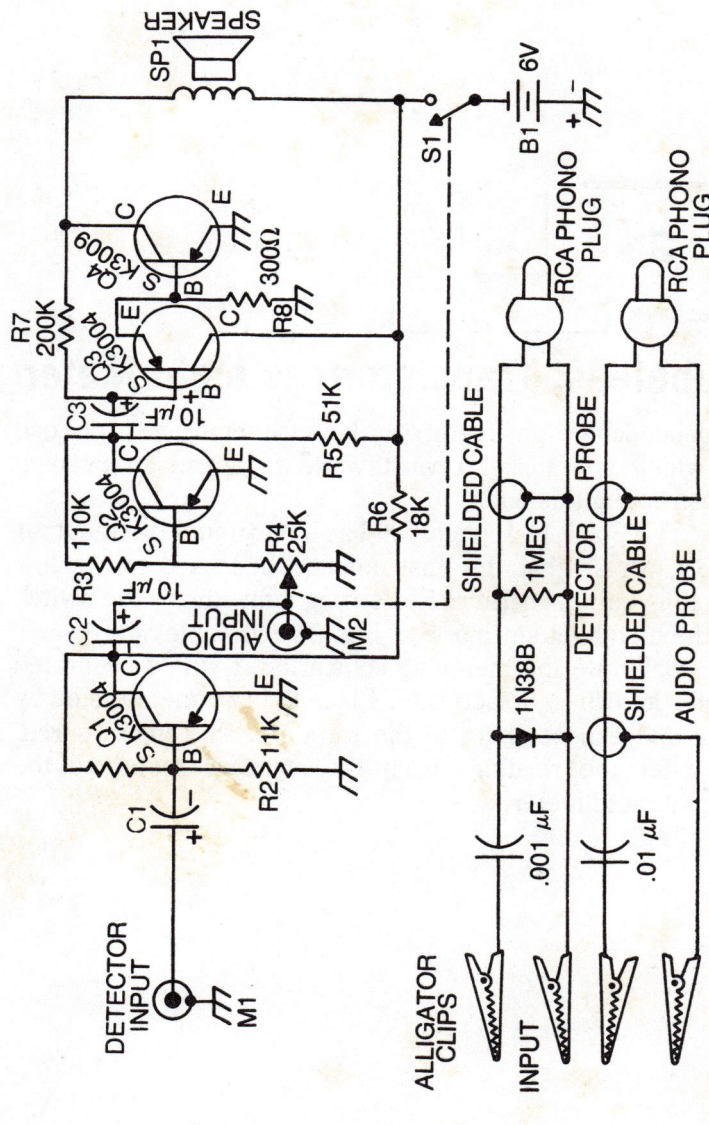

Fig. 33. Signal tracer circuit.

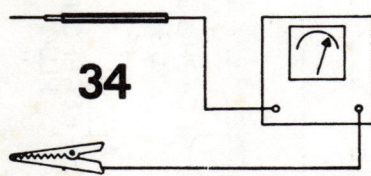

Tubeless, Transistorless Light Meter

A dependable light meter can have several uses, any one of which will make it worthwhile to spend an evening constructing this one.

The Solar 11-L photocell has a maximum rated output of 12 mA so that this instrument when used on its low range is quite sensitive. For strong light, throw the switch to the high light setting. See Fig. 34 and Table 34.

Calibrate the meter by comparing it with a calibrated meter known to be accurate. Place the two meters side by side and expose them to the same variable light source. Transfer the readings from the standard meter to the uncalibrated meter.

Table 34. Parts List for Tubeless, Transistorless Light Meter.

Item No.	Description
M1	0-1 milliammeter.
M2	Photocell (Solar 11-L or equiv.).
R1	1k potentiometer.
S1	Spdt switch.

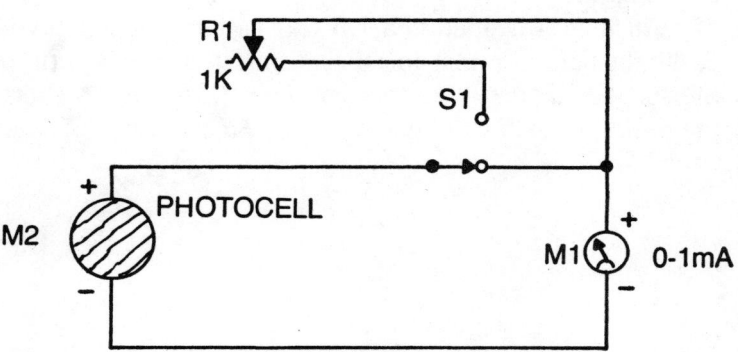

Fig. 34. Light meter circuit.

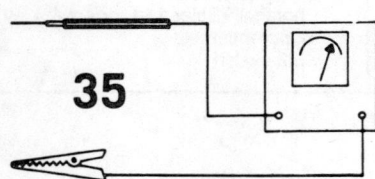

Simple Short Detector

If you haven't built the shockless continuity tester yet (Project #1) and need to test for a short circuit in a hurry, you can put this simple short detector together in a very few minutes.

All that is needed is a 1.5 volt battery and a 1.5 volt flashlight bulb. To test for shorts, just touch each side of the suspected point with the test leads. If there is a short, the flashlight bulb will light. See Fig. 35 and Table 35.

Table 35. Parts List for Simple Short Detector.

Item No.	Description
B1	1.5-volt battery.
M1	1.5-volt flashlight bulb.

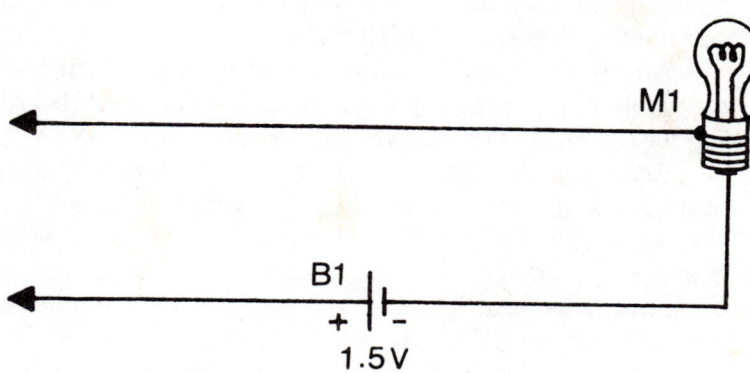

Fig. 35. Short detector circuit.

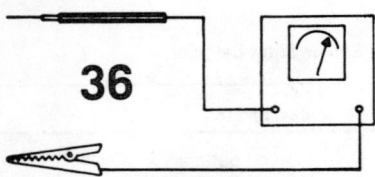

Transistor Frequency Standard

A frequency standard is useful for many purposes. For instance, a SWL is trying to identify a real DX station. How is it done if the calibration of the receiver is not really accurate? Many hams avoid the band edges because they are afraid they may accidentally be outside the specific ham band and thus receive a citation from the FCC.

A frequency standard can be used to solve these problems as well as others because it will generate a signal every 100 kHz, or 1/10 MHz.

All of the components for this unit are so small that the whole thing can be put together on a bit of Vectorboard and tucked inside the receiver case if you desire.

After construction, connect to the receiver antenna terminal as shown. You will hear a signal every 10 kHz. Now adjust L1, the variable inductance so that no sound is heard in the receiver. You may like a small audio sound or complete "zero beat." Both conditions you will be able to obtain by adjustment of L1.. See Fig. 36 and Table 36.

Table 36. Parts List for Transistor Frequency Standard.

Item No.	Description
C1	5—100-pF variable capacitor (Allied Radio No. 43B3776 or equiv.).
C2	430-pF capacitor.
C3	500-pF capacitor.
C4	.05-µF capacitor.
L1	6—35-mH adjustable rf choke.
B1	9-volt transistor battery.
Q1	SK3004 transistor.
R1	220k resistor.
R2	470-ohm resistor.
S1	Spst switch.
	100kHz crystal.

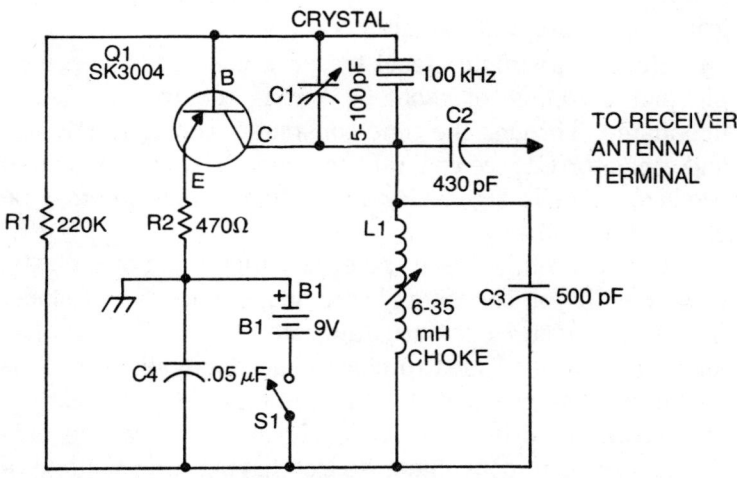

Fig. 36. Frequency standard circuit.

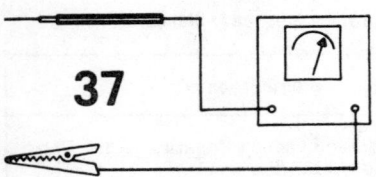

Neon-Lamp Signal Tracer

Much of present-day electronic gear produces sound whether it is a high-fidelity sound system, an ac-dc radio, a ham receiver or a television receiver. Each of these employs audio tubes or audio transistors, and troubleshooting these devices requires an audio generator. An audio generator can be quite simple as long as a small signal can be applied to the grid of an appropriate stage.

Here is a simple signal tracer which uses the principle that a voltage of about 90 Vdc is required to light a neon lamp. Through the time constant of resistors R1, R2, and capacitor C1, we can light the neon bulb at speeds that produce an audio signal. By adjusting R2, the tone may be changed to suit.

Construct this signal tracer in a metal box or a plastic container. If you choose a plastic box, connect all grounds. Insulated alligator clips are suggested for the B+ and B− leads. It is a good idea to color code these alligator clips by painting the grounnd clip black and the B+ clip red.

Power to drive this audio signal tracer can be borrowed from any convenient source having a dc voltage of 100 to 150 volts. You may be able to obtain the voltage needed from the piece of gear you are troubleshooting.

To use this unit, connect the ground clip to the chassis of the power source. Connect the B+ clip to 100 to 150 volts dc. Connect the ground terminal to the chassis of the unit being tested. Connect the audio output to the grid of the last tube before the speaker. Adjust the volume control so that the sound is just audible. Now connect the audio output terminal to the grid of the preceding stage. An increase in sound should be noted. If no sound is heard or there is a drop in volume, this is the faulty stage. Now check voltages and the components in this stage until the faulty one is found. See Fig. 37 and Table 37.

Table 37. Parts List for Neon-Lamp Signal Tracer.

Item No.	Description
C1	.001-μF capacitor.
C2, C3	.03-μF capacitors.
M1	NE-2E neon lamp.
R1	1.5meg resistor.
R2	1.5meg potentiometer.
R3	7.5k potentiometer.

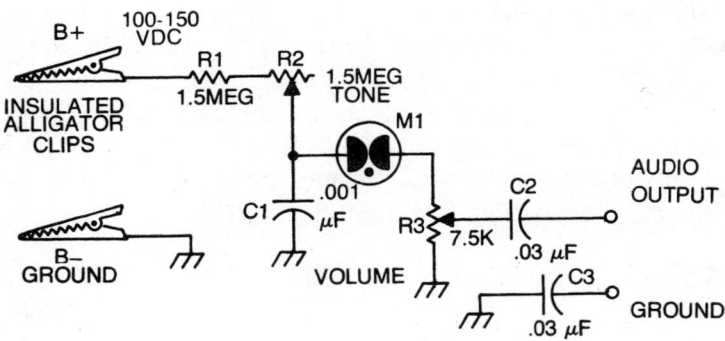

Fig. 37. Signal tracer circuit.

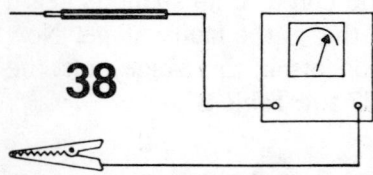

Miniature Voltmeter

Many times in electronic testing it is not necessary to know exactly how many volts are present at a certain test point. Quite often it is sufficient to know that voltage is present and the approximate amount.

This little voltmeter has no meter but depends on the use of a 25¢ neon lamp. The rest of the components are probably available and the complete unit may be constructed in any small plastic box.

The NE-2E neon lamp will light when a potential of 65 volts ac or more or about 100 volts dc is applied. When used in the dc position, capacitor C1 is charged through resistor R1. When the "firing voltage" of the lamp is reached, it will light momentarily. The higher the dc voltage being tested, the more rapid will be the rate at which blinking occurs. By noting the number of blinks per second, it is possible to estimate fairly accurately the dc voltage being tested.

When the meter is set in the ac position, the NE-2E lamp will be on continuously. It will be necessary to estimate differences in ac voltages by judging the intensity of lamp illumination. See Fig. 38 and Table 38.

Table 38. Parts List for Miniature Voltmeter.

Item No.	Description
C1	.47-µF capacitor.
M1	NE-2E neon lamp.
R1	8.2meg resistor.
R2	120k resistor.
S1	Spdt switch.

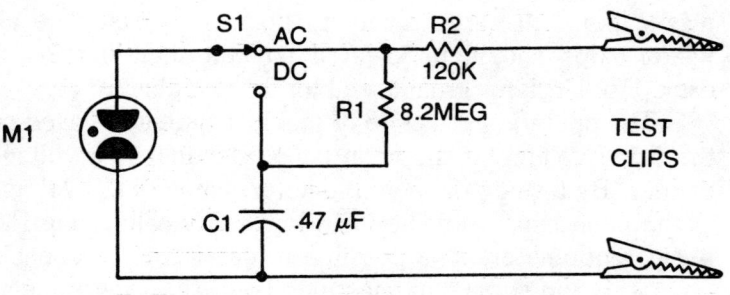

Fig. 38. Voltmeter circuit.

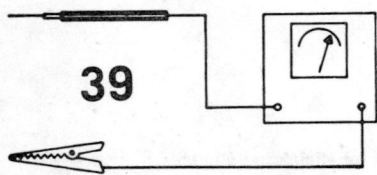

39

AC-DC Voltmeter

Would you like to be able to determine ac or dc voltages accurately by using a handful of spare parts? If so, read on—this is for you.

As in the previously shown instrument, the heart of this one is the 25¢ neon lamp. The NE-2E will light when 65-60 volts ac, or approximately 100 volts dc, is applied to its terminal.

The other components shown are probably already available, but, if not, their cost will be very little. A small plastic box will serve nicely to hold the parts. The alligator clips should be painted so that identification is easy. Use black for ground, red for dc, and blue for ac.

The operating principle of this instrument is based on the firing voltage of the neon lamp. Our unit is a voltage divider. By turning the potentiometer, we vary the voltage at the neon lamp until the lamp lights. By calibrating R2, the potentiometer, it is possible to determine reasonably accurately the voltage in question. To use this instrument, connect the ground clip to the chassis ground, then connect the voltage to the ac or dc clip as required. Start with the potentiometer R2 all the way down and gradually turn it until the lamp lights. Read the voltage from the previously calibrated scale.

A friend who has a variable-voltage power supply and voltmeter will probably be glad to let you use his equipment for calibration. It will be necessary to calibrate for both ac and dc, since the bulb does not "fire" at the same value in each case.

When connected to a dc voltage, it is always possible to determine polarity by observing which electrode lights. The lighted electrode is connected to negative polarity. Connected to ac voltage, both electrodes will light. See Fig. 39 and Table 39.

Table 39. Parts List for AC-DC Voltmeter.

Item No.	Description
C1	.15-μF capacitor.
M1	NE-2E neon pilot light.
R1, R3	120k resistor.
R2	1.5meg potentiometer.
	Three (3) insulated alligator clips.

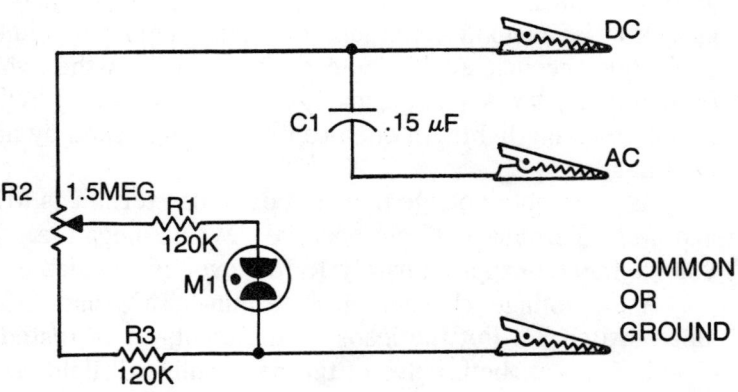

Fig. 39. AC-DC voltmeter circuit.

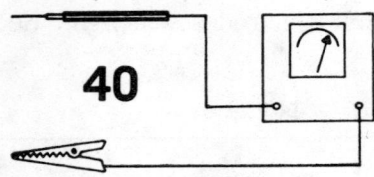

A Small Multitester

As the name implies, this is a multipurpose unit. You may use it as a capacitor checker, a variable-voltage power supply, a voltage checker, or a continuity tester.

The circuit is simple, and there are no critical elements involved. It should cost little to construct. Jacks M1, M2 and M3 are not specified. You may choose those which best fit your needs.

To use as a capacitor checker, connect a capacitor across terminals M1 and M2. Close the switch S1. If the capacitor is in good condition, the neop lamp will blink every few seconds. A shorted capacitor will show the light on continuously. A leaky capacitor will be indicated by a rapidly blinking light. An open capacitor is indicated by no light at all.

As a variable-voltage power supply, use terminals M1 and M3. Terminal M1 is positive; M3 is negative. A voltage range of approximately 15 to 90 volts is available.

As a voltage checker, use terminals M2 and M3. Open switch S1. Put the leads on the points to be tested. If ac is present, both poles of the neon bulb will light. Dc voltage will light only one pole. Voltages below 90 volts cannot be checked.

As a community checker, use M1 or M2. Close switch S1. Short the leads to M1 and M2. The lamp will glow. Now put the test leads across the circuit in question. If the circuit is not open, the bulb will glow. See Fig. 40 and Table 40.

Table 40. Parts List for Multitester.

Item No.	Description
C1	20-μF, 150-volt, electrolytic capacitor.
M1, M2, M3	Output jacks.
M4	NE-2E neon bulb.
R1	10-ohm, 2-watt resistor.
R2	51k resistor.
R3	15k, 10-watt wirewound potentiometer.
S1	Spst switch.
X1	Rectifier (GE-504A or equiv.).

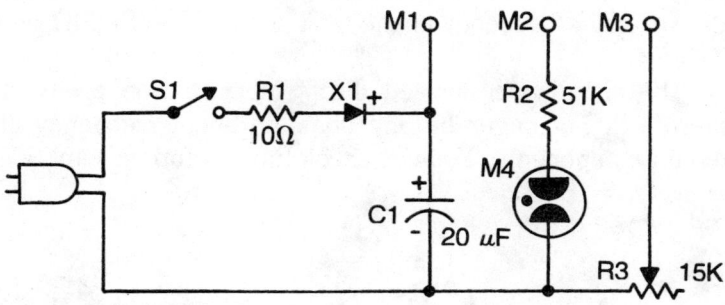

Fig. 40. Multitester circuit.

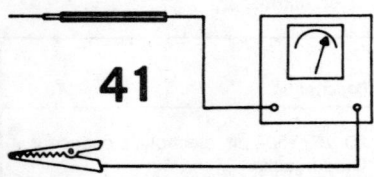

Radio Frequency Calibrator

This little device is just about the easiest project you can build. Do not let this mislead you. It is very useful.

The circuit, when connected to a "tank" circuit, is a transistor oscillator that will oscillate at a frequency between 3.5 to 40 MHz, depending on the frequency of the tank-circuit coil-and-capacitor combination. When this unit oscillates at a frequency as determined by the tank circuit, it radiates a small amount of rf energy which may be received on your communications receiver. Tune your receiver to the maximum signal and you can read directly the resonant frequency of the tank circuit. See Fig. 41 and Table 41.

If this device is used during construction projects, there will no longer be any question about frequency of circuit components. You can check them before assembly.

Table 41. Parts List for Radio Frequency Calibrator.

Item No.	Description
C1	.01-μF capacitor.
C2	24-pF capacitor.
B1	6-volt battery.
Q1	SK3008 transistor.
R1	680k resistor.
R2	1.2k resistor.

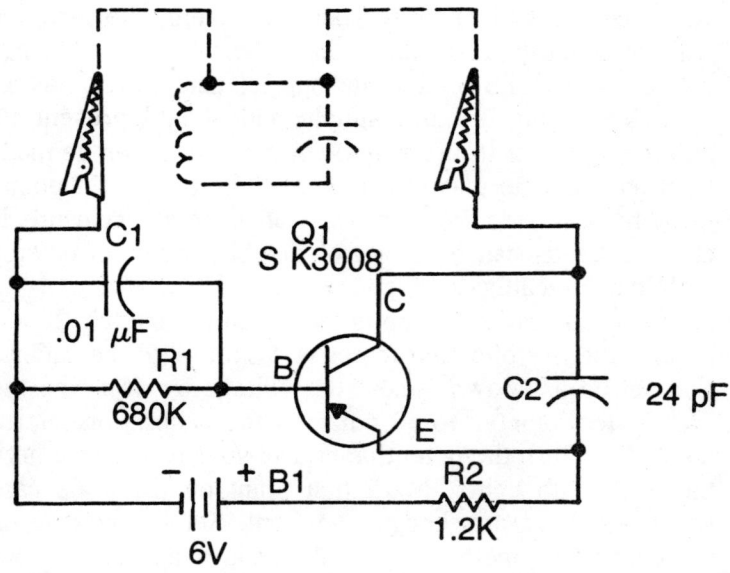

Fig. 41. Radio frequency calibration circuit.

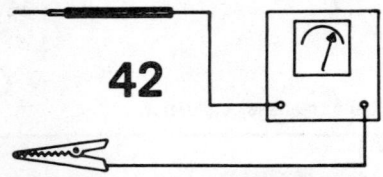

All-Around Multitester

How would you like to build a multimeter for measuring ac volts, dc volts, and resistance for just a few dollars? You may have all of the parts available; if so, your real cost is represented by labor. This unit will test ac voltages from 40 to 220 volts, dc voltages from 60 to 320 volts, and resistances from 8000 to 250,000 ohms.

The principle on which this multitester is based is the fact that the neon lamp NE-2E will not light until its "firing" voltage is reached. This varies from lamp to lamp, but since you will calibrate your instrument, the variation will not affect the accuracy of the instrument. This "firing" voltage is about 65 volts ac and approximately 90 volts dc.

The circuit is quite simple and should present no problem. The enclosure may be of metal or it can be made from an available plastic container. The three test points must be insulated from the case if a metal enclosure is chosen. Leads can be made of flexible wire, terminated with insulated alligator clips.

The calibration set-up is shown on the sketch. It will require the use of a multitester or VOM. With the calibration set-up as shown, adjust the voltage by adjusting the 750k potentiometer to 50 volts on the calibration instrument. Now turn the potentiometer of your instrument until the neon bulb lights. Mark that point on the scale card which you have attached to the front. Set the voltage on the calibration meter to 45 volts, and again adjust your tester until the neon bulb lights. Calibrate that point on the scale card. Proceed downward as far as possible and upward as far as possible. Dc readings will be 1.4 times the value of the ac readings. For example: 100 volts ac will correspond to 140 volts dc. A second scale can be constructed in this manner for dc. The ohms scale can be calibrated by putting known values of resistance between the ohms terminal and ground. You may start with the resistor in your spare-parts box. Additional values of resistance may be calibrated by putting two resistors in series. When the calibration is completed, you will have three concentric circles of values for ac volts, dc volts, and resistance. See Fig. 42 and Table 42.

Table 42. Parts List for All-Around Multitester.

Item No.	Description
M1	NE-2E neon lamp.
R1	24k resistor.
R2	100k potentiometer.
S1	Spst switch.
T1	Power transformer: primary, 117 Vac; secondary, 125 Vac at 15 mA (Allied Radio No. 54B1410 or equiv.).

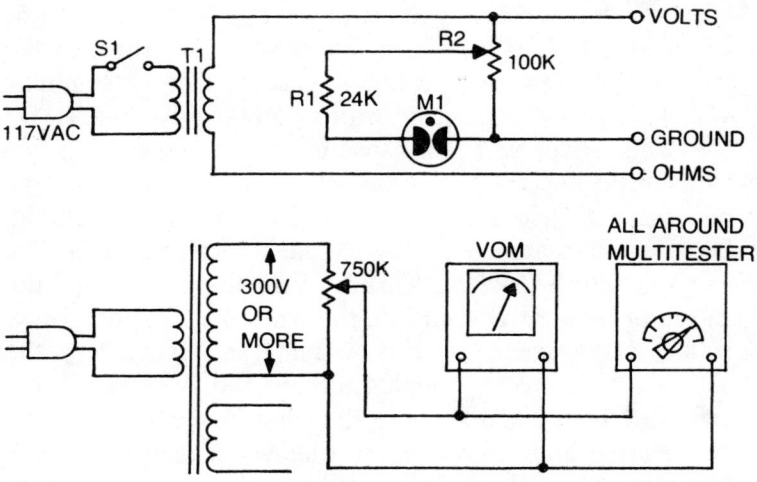

Fig. 42. All-around multitester circuit.

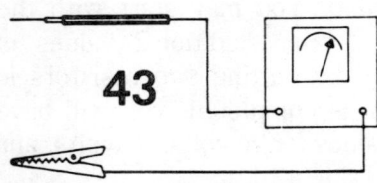

Junk-box Capacitor Tester

Almost everyone has a VOM or VTVM which can be used for checking resistances, voltage, etc., but capacitors are something else again. To complicate the problem further, there are several methods of identifying the capacitance. Some capacitors have colored bars; others have colored dots, etc., so the neophyte may have quite a few capacitors on hand that he is reluctant to use. If this is your problem, here is the answer.

The parts to construct this valuable adjunct to the home electronics workshop are not expensive. The tester may be constructed with a layout to suit the cabinet of your choice. Keep T1 and the ac line feeding the input as remote as possible from the balance of the wiring. The accuracy of this tester will depend partly on capacitors C1, C2, and C3. Use capacitors as close as possible to the values specified. If you have not way of determining values, purchase capacitors with ±5 percent tolerance.

This tester will test capacitors from 100 microfarads to as little as 100 picofarads. For calibration, it will be necessary to use capacitors of known value. If possible, borrow a capacitance decade. Make the calibration set-up as shown in the sketch. Turn on both the VTVM and the capacitor tester. Disconnect the known capacitor. Now, rotate R1 to see if there is a "null" as indicated by the VTVM. If there is, unplug either the VTVM or the capacitor tester and reverse the plug in the wall, but do not reverse both. Now, insert a known capacitance at the test terminals and rotate R1 until a "null" is evident. Mark the proper scale at this point. Proceed for the balance of the calibration. Mark the scales × 10, × 0.1 and ×0.001. In using this instrument, proceed as you would in reading resistances. The value indicated will be multiplied by ×10, ×0.1, or ×0.001. See Fig. 43 and Table 43.

Table 43. Parts List for Junk-Box Capacitor Tester.

Item No.	Description
C1	10-μF, 50-volt, electrolytic capacitor (Mallory 10E50 or equiv.).
C2	.1-μF tubular capacitor.
C3	.001-μF silver mica capacitor.
R1	7.5k potentiometer.
S1	Spst switch.
S2	Single-pole, 3-position, nonshorting switch (Oak No. 399195-29 or equiv.).
T1	6.3-Vac filament transformer (Allied Radio No. 54B2323 or equiv.).

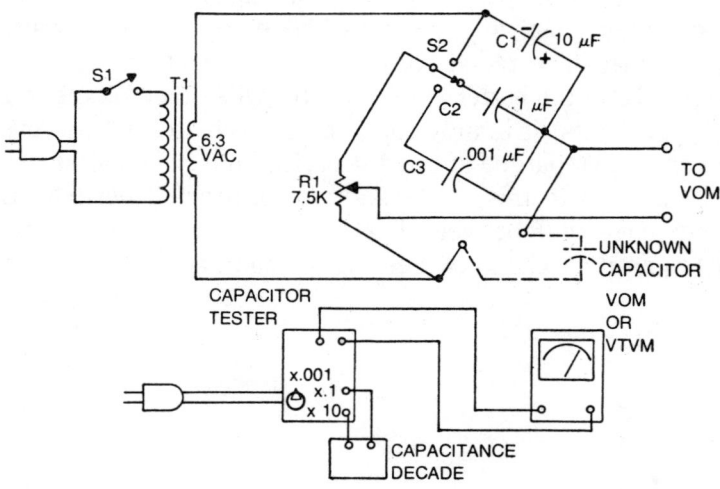

Fig. 43. Capacitor tester circuit.

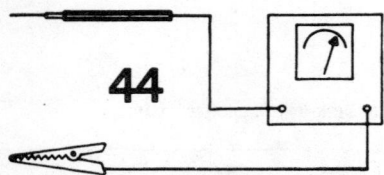

Flashlight Battery Rejuvenator

Batteries are becoming an increasing item of expense since so much is being done with transistors. Would you like to reduce this expense? Here is how you can do it at little cost.

The parts needed are not expensive or critical. Construction can be in any convenient container, such as a small plastic box. The terminals should be identified for polarity by marking + and − at the appropriate position on the box.

To use, connect a battery across the terminals. Be sure that the proper polarity is observed. The ¼-inch diameter post at the top of the battery is the positive terminal. The metal battery case is negative. Check the voltage of the battery periodically. When the voltage is 1.6 to 1.7 volts, it is fully charged. Some batteries, however, cannot be charged above 1.4 or 1.5 volts, even after being connected to this rejuvenator for protracted periods. Experience will be your best guide in the length of time required for charging. See Fig. 44 and Table 44.

Table 44. Parts List for Flashlight Battery Rejuvenator.

Item No.	Description
R1	1.5k resistor.
S1	Dpst switch.
T1	Transistor output transformer used as a step-down transformer (Argonne AR-143 or equiv.).
X1	Rectifier (GE-504A or equiv.).

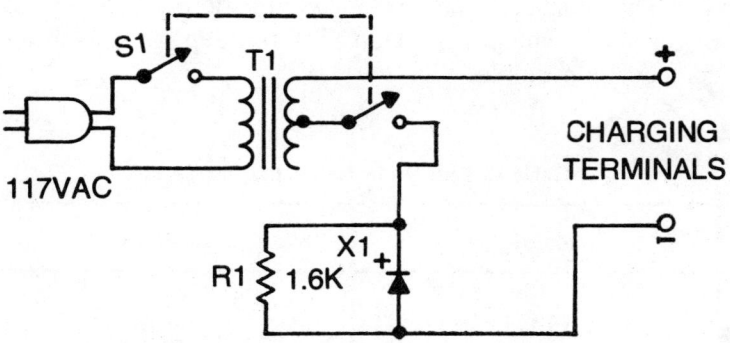

Fig. 44. Flashlight battery rejuvenator circuit.

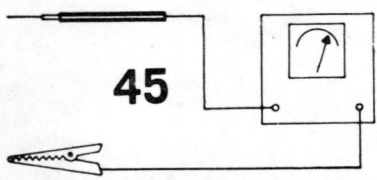

Multipurpose Comparator

There are many times when an accurately calibrated meter is not needed. Often we need to know whether a particular stage is "working" or not. With this particular piece of home-constructed gear it will be possible to answer such questions as well as to be able to compare relative values of power.

This comparator is actually two units: the meter and its associated parts, and the probe. The battery, transistor, etc., can be mounted right on the back of the meter case. The probe will need a length of flexible shielded cable for bringing the rectified signal to the meter. See Fig. 45 and Table 45.

The shape of the probe will be determined by the materials of which it is made. Try to keep it as small and compact as possible.

Table 45. Parts List for Multipurpose Comparator.

Item No.	Description
C1	.015-μF capacitor.
B1	1.5-volt battery.
M1	0-1 milliammeter.
Q1	SK3003 transistor.
R1	360k resistor.
R2	20k resistor.
R3	27k resistor.
X1	1N38B diode.

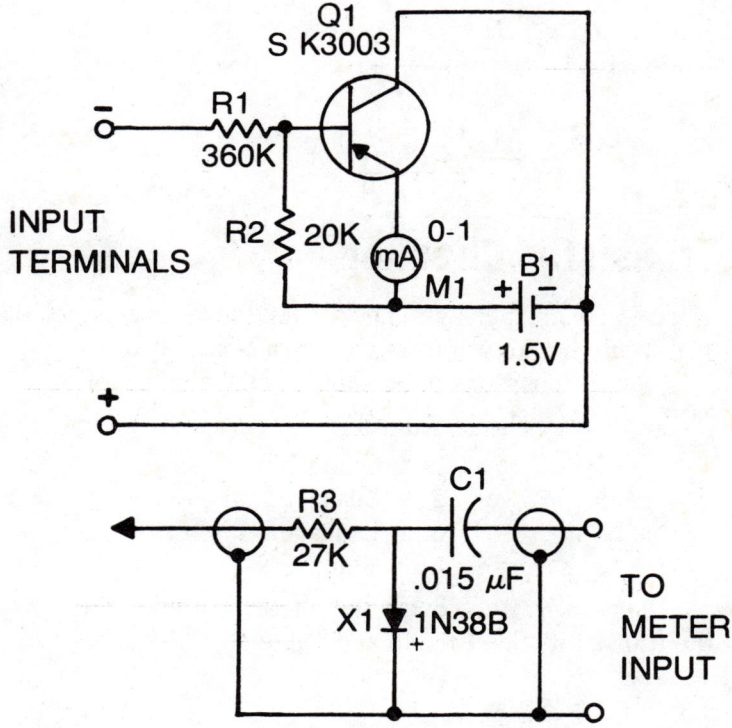

Fig. 45. Multipurpose comparator circuit.

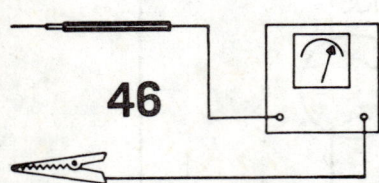

Transistor Checker

Here is an inexpensive checker for those transistors that you would like to use from your spare-parts box.

Switch positions of S1 should be labeled as follows:

>   *Switch Position*
>   1   Gain PNP
>   2   Leakage PNP
>   3   Leakage NPN
>   4   Gain NPN

Generally, the lower the meter reading, the better the transistor. See Fig. 46 and Table 46.

Table 46. Parts List for Transistor Checker.

Item No.	Description
B1	6-volt battery.
M1	0-1 milliammeter.
R, R2	620k resistors.
S1	3-pole, 4-position switch (Mallory 3134J or equiv.).
S2	Spst switch.

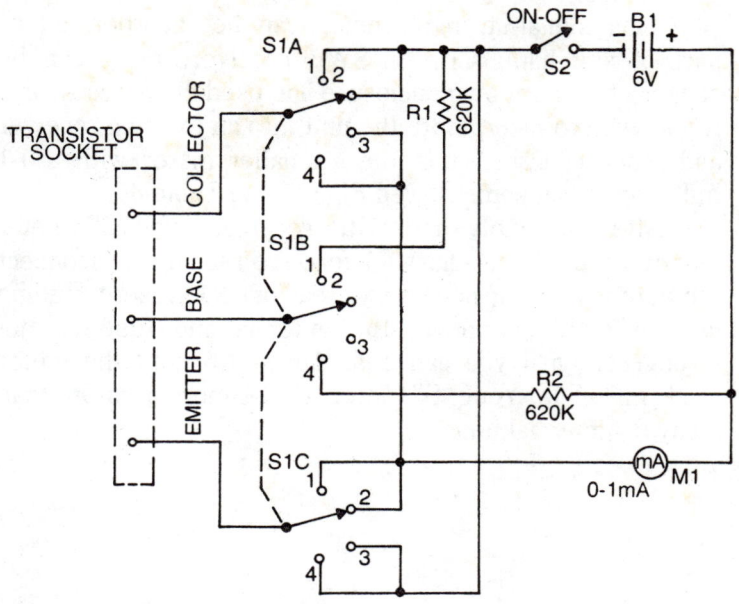

Fig. 46. Transistor checker circuit.

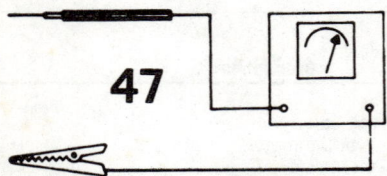

Add A Signal-Strength Meter

There are many communications receivers that are not equipped with signal-strength meters. It is not at all accurate to try to estimate signal strength by listening because the gain control is not usually set at the same place twice.

This signal-strength meter can be incorporated as part of any ham, CB, or SWL receiver, or it can be constructed in its own enclosure and used as an accessory. If you wish to incorporate the unit into an existing receiver and space is tight, substitue a smaller meter with a 0-1 milliampere movement. See Fig. 47 and Table 47.

After assembly and with receiver and "S" meter circuit warmed up, adjust R1 for zero reading. Disconnect the antenna and, if necessary, readjust R1 to zero reading on the meter. Connect the antenna and tune to the strongest signal you can find. Adjust R5 until the meter reads full scale. Your "S" meter will be more accurate than many commercial units.

Table 47. Parts List for Signal Strength Meter.

Item No.	Description
C1, C2	.01-µF capacitors.
M1	0-1 milliammeter (Allied Radio No. 52B8012 or equiv.).
R1, R5	25k potentiometers.
R2	2meg resistor.
R3, R7	10meg resistors.
R4, R6	3.3k resistors.
V1	5963 tube.

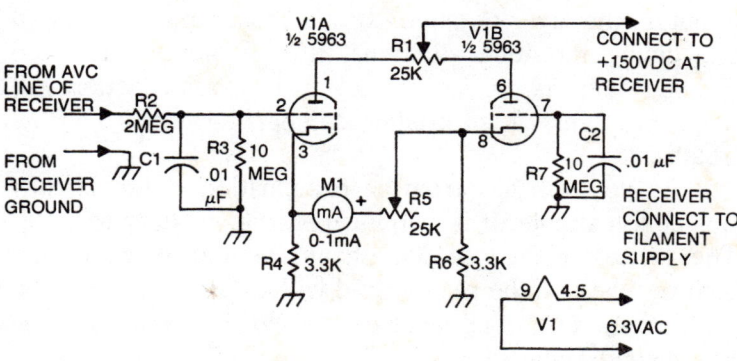

Fig. 47. Signal-strength meter circuit.

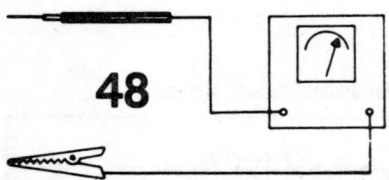

Radio-TV Tube Rejuvenator

This is not strictly a piece of test gear; however, it is so closely allied, it has been included. It is used to rejuvenate tubes which fall below the required level of performance and would ordinarily be discarded.

A tube with use eventually builds up a coating of inert oxide ash on the cathode. The process usually requires months, sometimes years. When the coating becomes heavy enough, cathode emission drops to the point that the tube is no longer serviceable. By operating the tube heater at about 35 percent above its rated voltage for 10 to 12 minutes, the layer of oxide ash may sometimes be burned off, giving the tube additional life. In some tubes the cathode oxide is, so far, "gone" that no rejuvenation will help; however, a surprising number benefit from this treatment.

As you will see from an examination of the circuit, this unit is simple. It is also inexpensive and easy to build. The leads attached to M4 should be left long so that picture tubes can be rejuvenated without removal from the TV cabinet. Cut off all leads except No. 1 and No. 12. See Fig. 48 and Table 48.

To use the rejuvenator, plug in a tube, with the switch set for the test position. The neon lamp should glow. If it does not, the tube is burned out. Consult the tube manual for heater current data and set switch S1 to the appropriate setting. It may be necessary to give the tube two rejuvenating cycles. Not all tubes respond but you will be surprised how many do.

Table 48. Parts List for Radio-TV Tube Rejuvenator.

Item No.	Description
M1	7-pin miniature tube socket.
M2	Octal tube socket.
M3	9-pin miniature tube socket.
M4	Picture tube socket with leads.
M5	NE-2E neon lamp.
R1	51k resistor.
R2	6.8-ohm, 2-watt resistor.
R3	13-ohm, 2-watt resistor.
R4	27-ohm, 2-watt resistor.
S1	5-position switch (Allied Radio No. 56B4350 or equiv.) 4 positions used.
T1	12.6-volt filament transformer (Allied Radio No. 54B1420 or equiv.).

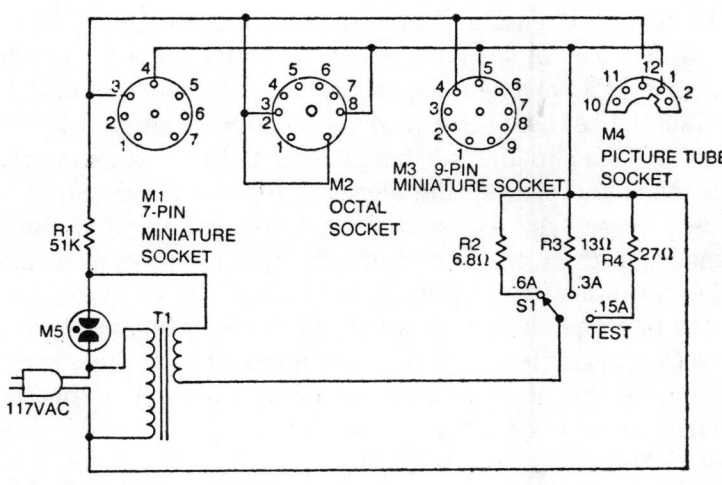

Fig. 48. Tube rejuvenator circuit.

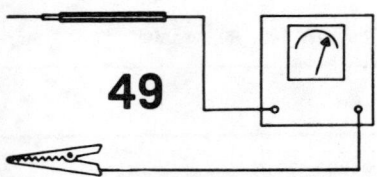

One-Transistor Signal Tracer

The signal tracer is one of the most useful of all pieces of test gear. A signal tracer permits you to listen to the signal of a radio receiver or an amplifier at a particular stage. The unit shown here is not a complete signal tracer. It must be connected to the phono jack of a working receiver. In this manner the cost of building this piece of test gear has been kept to a minimum.

There is nothing critical about this circuit that would cause problems. Use the usual care in construction. Do not sober the transistor in place unless you use a heat sink to prevent the heat from being transmitted through the leads to the transistor. See Fig. 49 and Table 49.

To use this signal tracer, plug its output into the phono jack of a working receiver. Turn on the switch. Tune the set being tested to a strong local station. Clip the ground lead to the set being tested. Now, begin at the antenna and pick up the signal at the input and output of each stage. This is easily done by touching first the grid and then the plate of each stage. As you proceed, it may be necessary to turn down the gain of the receiver. You will find one stage with no signal, a distorted signal, or a weak signal. Here is the faulty stage. One of the components of this stage will be defective. Check them one by one until you find the faulty one.

Table 49. Parts List for One-Transistor Signal Tracer.

Item No.	Description
C1	.001-µF disc ceramic capacitor.
C2, C3	1.0-µF, 25-volt, miniature electrolytic capacitor.
V1	9-volt battery.
Q1	SK3004 transistor.
R1	1.1meg resistor.
R2	1.5meg potentiometer.
S1	Spst switch.
X1	1N38B diode.

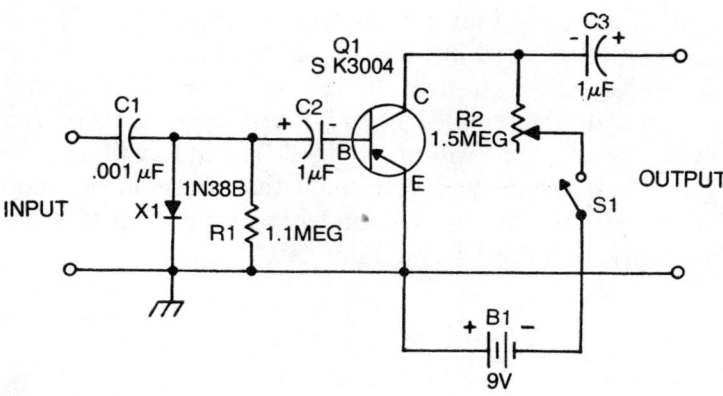

Fig. 49. Signal tracer circuit.

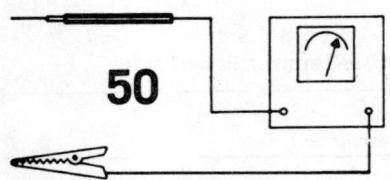

50

Handy Fuse Saver

Have you reached that point in a construction project where you have spent a great deal of time and the unit is now ready for tryout? What if there is a serious short or other faulty wiring? Several days of work can be ruined in an instant.

Here is a little device that is designed to solve the above problem. Plug a light bulb of the approximate wattage of the device being tested into M1. Make sure that S1 is open. Plug the device in question into M2 and insert the line cord into a wall outlet. If there is *no* short, the light bulb will light to full brilliance. If a short is present, the bulb will light to full brilliance. If there is an open circuit, there will be no light. The bulb will not even become warm. If you determine that there is no short, close S1 and the device under test may be operated normally. See Fig. 50 and Table 50.

Table 50. Parts List for Handy Fuse Saver.

Item No.	Description
M1	117-Vac socket for household light bulb.
M2	117-Vac receptacle.
S1	Spst switch.

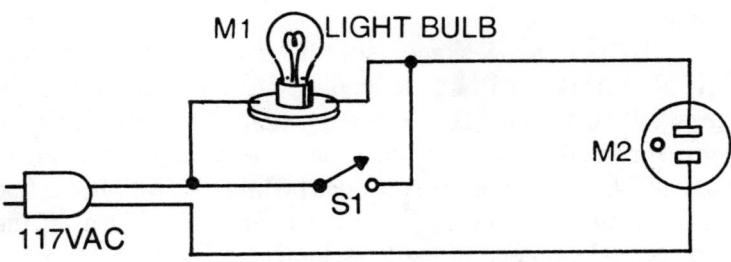

Fig. 50. Fuse saver circuit.

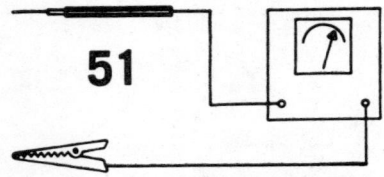

Professional Dual-Meter Transistor Checker

Sometimes brand new transistors are not good. Sometimes, if we are a little careless, they are damaged during construction of a project. So, you put together a piece of equipment and it does not work; you recheck all the wiring and the problem is not the wiring. Then what do you do? Well, here is a tester that will answer your next questions. It will tell you if the transistors are good or not.

This tester will measure the current gain and the collector-to-base leakage. Do not use it if you have a transistor rated at 5 milliamperes or less maximum collector current. You will have to come up with some other means to test these low power transistors.

Two meters are incorporated in this tester. You will be able to check base and collector current at the same time.

To test for leakage, set the switch S2 for leakage NPN or leakage PNP, depending on the transistor to be tested. Connect the emitter lead for any leakage measurement. Now, advance the potentiometer R3. Leakage will be evident if a reading can be taken on M2. If you find no leakage, proceed to test for current gain. Turn off the power and connect all leads as indicated on the schematic. Check the transistor specifications for the maximum collector current. This current is read on M2. *Do not exceed this figure for any reason*. Set R3 for full off and turn on the tester. Set the potentiometer so that M2 is reading below the maximum allowable collector current. Divide the collector current by the base current. This is the gain of the transistor. You will now be able to test your transistors. See Fig. 51 and Table 51.

Table 51. Parts List for Professional Dual-Meter Transistor Checker.

Item No.	Description
C1, C2, C3, C4	100-μF, 15-volt, electrolytic capacitors.
F1	.5-A fuse.
M1	0-1 milliammeter (Allied Radio No. 52B7609 or equiv.).
M2	0-100 milliammeter (Allied Radio No. 52B7604 or equiv.).
R1, R2	30-ohm resistors.
R3	150k potentiometer.
R4	6.2k resistor.
R5	1.1k one-watt resistor.
S1	Spst switch.
S2	Four-pole, four-position switch (Allied Radio No. 56B5071 or equiv.).
T1	6.3-volt filament transformer (Allied Radio No. 54B3715 or equiv.).
X1, X2	1N158 diodes.

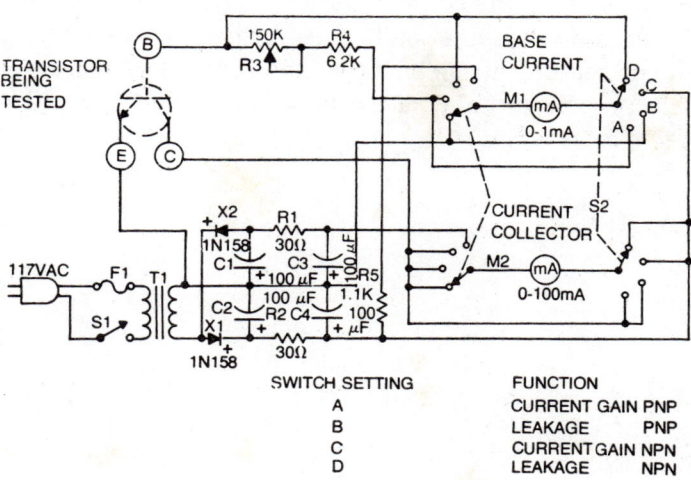

SWITCH SETTING	FUNCTION
A	CURRENT GAIN PNP
B	LEAKAGE PNP
C	CURRENT GAIN NPN
D	LEAKAGE NPN

Fig. 51 Transistor checker circuit.

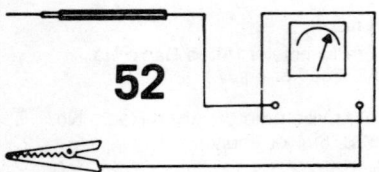

Low-Voltage Silicon Rectifier Tester

Many common low-voltage silicon rectifiers (such as the SK3030, etc.) can easily be tested for good/bad and open/short conditions on the simple tester shown in the accompanying diagram. The checker should not be used, however, on the 1N270 types or the 1N34A-variety germaniums.

In operation, when a diode is placed in the circuit where X1 is shown (with S1 closed) the bulb should light. If you reverse the battery, the bulb should immediately be extinguished. If the bulb doesn't light either way, the silicon rectifier is open. If the bulb comes on regardless of battery polarity, the diode is shorted. See Fig. 52 and Table 52.

Table 52. Parts List for Low-Voltage Silicon Rectifier Tester.

Item No.	Description
M1	Pilot bulb, Type No. 49 (60mA, 2-volts)
B1	6-volt battery.
R1	75-ohm resistor.
S1	Spst switch.
X1	Low-voltage silicon rectifier under test.

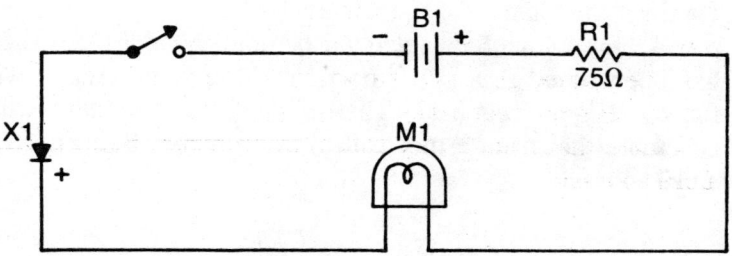

Fig. 52. Silicon rectifier tester.

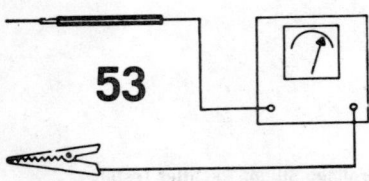

Transistor Metronome

Here is a pleasant evening project that will result in a metronome that may be useful for the children's musical education.

This circuit can be constructed in a small plastic box as the largest components are the battery and L1. Coil L1 is made by random winding 675 turns of No. 25 enamel covered wire on a ¼-inch bolt. At 475 turns, bare the wire and solder a tap for later connection into the circuit and continue the balance of the winding.

When completed, set it on or quite near a radio that has been tuned to a silent portion of the band. Adjust R1 for the timing required. The sound from the radio will resemble that from a mechanical metronome. See Fig. 53 and Table 53.

Table 53. Parts List for Transistor Metronome.

Item No.	Description
C1	30-μF, 12-volt electrolytic capacitor.
C2	.01-μF capacitor.
L1	See text.
B1	4.5-volt battery.
Q1	2N228 transistor.
R1	1meg potentiometer with switch.
R2	6800-ohm resistor.
S1	Part of R1.

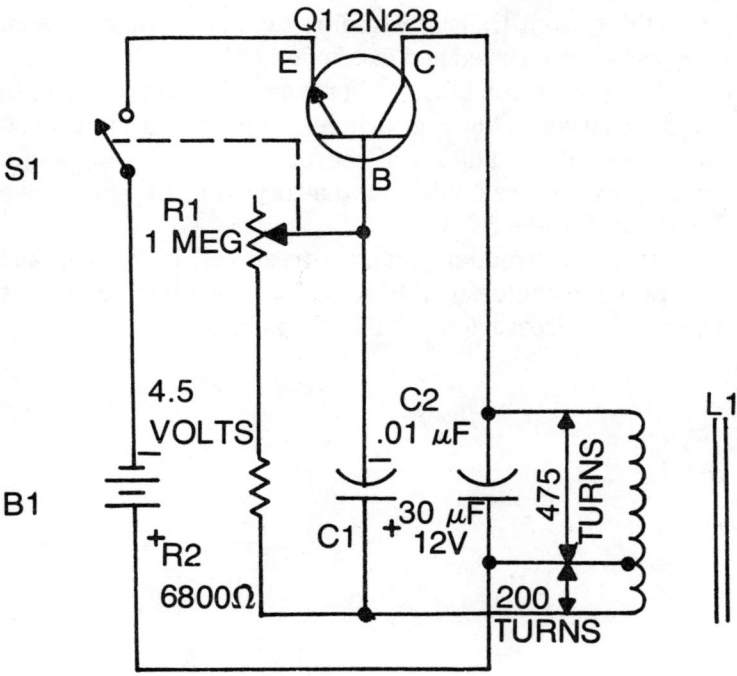

Fig. 53. Transistor metronome circuit.

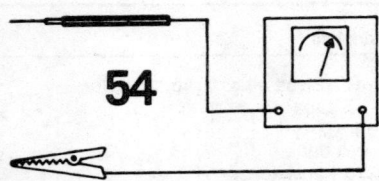

Flashlight Cell Tester/Charger

The use of flashlight cells as a low voltage source of power seems to increase from year to year. They are used in everything from transistor radios to toys. Within reason, they can be recharged and used over and over.

Here is a combination for you who would want to build a charger. This one includes a meter that allows you to observe the condition of the battery just by flipping a switch, without removing the battery from the clips. See Fig. 54 and Table 54.

After construction, insert a fresh cell in the clip and calibrate the meter to full scale by adjustment of R2. It will not be necessary to adjust R2 again.

Table 54. Parts List for Flashlight Cell Tester/Charger.

Item No.	Description
M1	0-100 milliammeter (Allied Radio No. 52B7619 or equiv.).
R1	750-ohm, 2-watt potentiometer.
R2	10-ohm, 10-watt potentiometer.
R3	300-ohm, ½-watt resistor.
S1	4pdt switch. (Allied Radio No. 56B4085 or equiv.).
T1	6.3-volt filament transformer.
X1	1N38B diode.

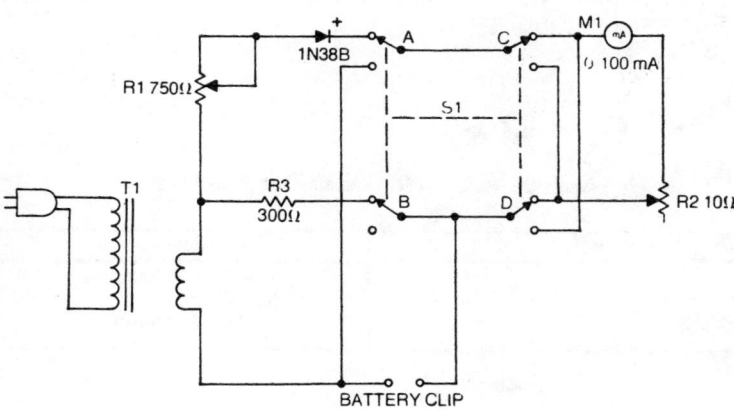

Fig. 54. Flashlight cell tester/charger circuit.

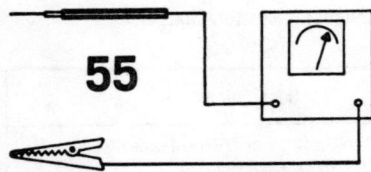

55

Filament-Type Tube Tester

Many radios and television sets have the tube filaments in a series string. Trying to quickly find the one that has failed is about as troublesome as determining which is the faulty lamp when the string of Christmas tree lights goes out.

Here is a tester that will check the filaments of these types of tubes and will also test fuses and pilot lamps. See Fig. 55 and Table 55.

Table 55. Parts List for Filament-Type Tube Tester.

Item No.	Description
B1	Two 1.5-volt batteries.
M1	No. 49 lamp.
	Sockets as shown.

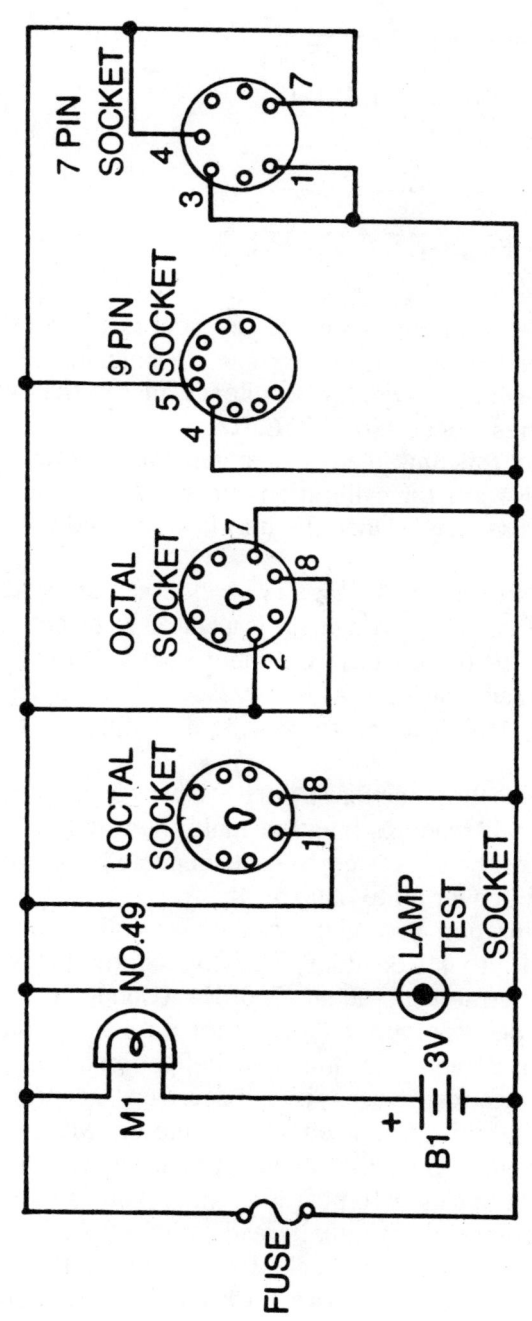

Fig. 55. Tube tester circuit.

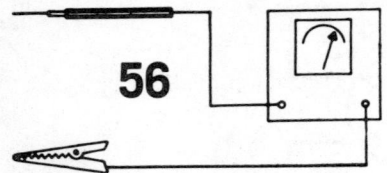

Diode Frequency Meter

A frequency meter is one of the necessary items of test gear needed by the electronic technician. Here is a direct-reading diode-type frequency meter that will read frequencies from 30 to 5000 hertz.

Build this unit in any convenient case. Potentiometers R1 and R4 are for calibration and should not be mounted on the front panel. Once the unit is calibrated do not touch them.

An alternating voltage is applied across either C1 or C2. The current through the capacitor is directly proportional to the frequency of the input signal. If the frequency is increased, the current is increased. The diodes X2 and X3 rectify this current to provide dc output for the meter M2.

S1 is the function switch. When it is in the ×10 position, all readings must be multiplied by ten. To calibrate, it will be necessary to have an audio generator whose range will cover 30 to 5000 hertz.

Calibration procedure can be as follows: With unit switched into ×1 position, R2 fully counterclockwise, and audio generator at about 500 Hz (Connected to unit's input), adjust potentiometer R2 for a midscale reading on M1. With R4 adjust for full-scale deflection of M2.

Key to calibration is to decrease generator's frequency while noting effect on meter M2. Once accomplished, repeat the above procedure with a 5000-Hz input with unit in ×10 position. Note: You can keep M1 at centerscale (25A) by simply readjusting R2 periodically.

Linearity can be checked by noting meter indication when switching from ×1 to ×10; for example, 300 Hz and

Table 56. Parts List for Diode Frequency Meter.

Item No.	Description
C1	.01-μF capacitor.
C2	.1-μF capacitor.
F1	1/8-A fuse and holder.
M1	0-50 microammeter (Allied Radio No. 52B7201 or equiv.).
M2	0-1 milliammeter (Allied Radio No. 52B8012 or equiv.).
R1, R4	25k potentiometers.
R2	100k, 2-watt potentiometer.
R3	240k resistor.
S1	Spdt switch.
X1, X2, X3	1N38B diodes.

3000 Hz should appear in the same place on the meter. If they do not, alter the value of C1 until the "times ten" ratio appears as desired. Once all of the preceding steps have been done, the meter can be relettered to read 0 through 500. See Fig. 56 and Table 56.

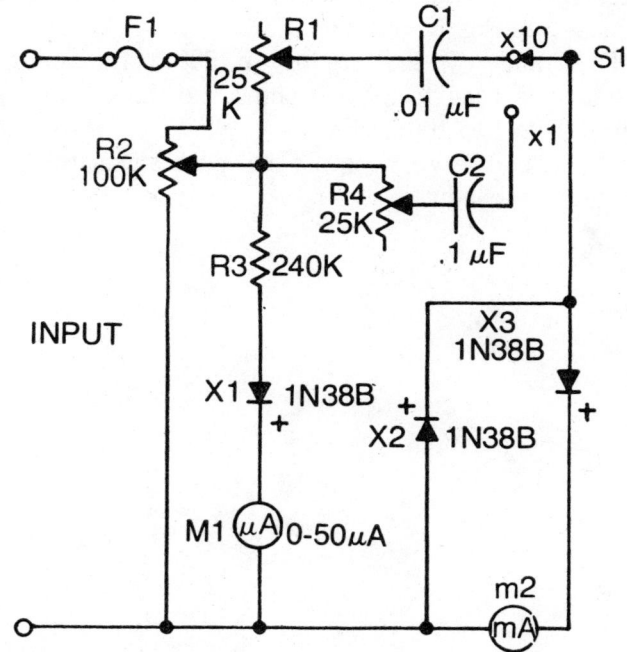

Fig. 56. Frequency meter circuit.

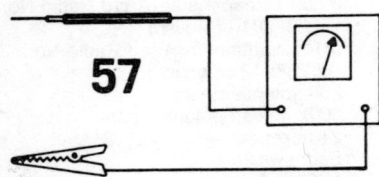

Miniature VOM

Here is a simple volt-ohm-milliammeter you can build and calibrate yourself. If you use care in choosing the components and constructing the unit, it can be made quite small. You will note that multiple jacks are used for various ranges rather than bulky and sometimes complex switches. See Fig. 57 and Table 57.

This unit will indicate up to 500 volts ac or dc. Resistance is read to 30,000 ohms and direct current is metered from 1 to 100 milliamps.

The circuit is very simple and self explanatory, as a brief study will show.

Table 57. Parts List for Miniature VOM.

Item No.	Description
M1	0-1 milliammeter.
B1	1.5-volt battery.
R1	100-ohm resistor.
R2	10-ohm resistor.
R3	4k resistor.
R4	360k resistor.
R5	100k resistor.
R6	36k resistor.
R7	10k resistor.
R8	150k resistor.
R9	43k resistor.
R10	15k resistor.
R11	5.1k resistor.
R12	2k potentiometer.
S1, S2	Spst switches.
X1, X2	1N34A diodes.

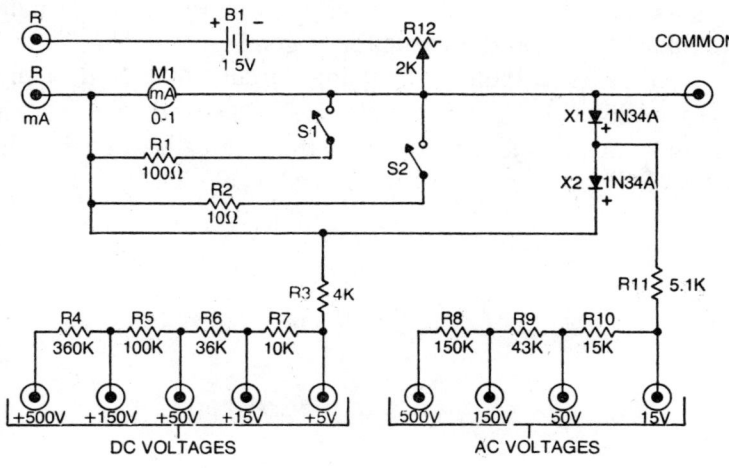

Fig. 57. Miniature VOM circuit.

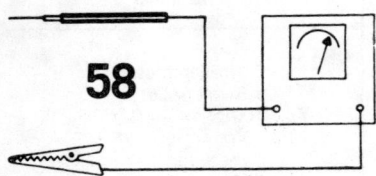

Capacitor Leakage Checker

A leaking capacitor can be very difficult to find and sometimes almost impossible to test with the usual tools available to the home experimenter, radio ham, or CB'er.

Here is an easy-to-construct capacitor checker that will do an excellent job. To use it, one end of the capacitor must be disconnected from the circuit. Connect the test leads and throw the switch. A small amount of leakage is indicated by repeated blinking of the neon bulb. If the bulb lights and stays on, the capacitor is shorted. If the bulb blinks only once, the capacitor is good.

This is a voltage-doubling circuit that will apply around 250 volts to the capacitor being checked. Construct it in a plastic box and *be careful* with the test leads when S1 is in the "ON" position. See Fig. 58 and Table 58.

Table 58. Parts List for Capacitor Leakage Checker.

Item No.	Description
C1, C2	8-μF, 250-volt electrolytic capacitors.
M1	NE51 neon bulb.
R1	3k resistor.
R2, R3	110k resistor.
S1	Spdt switch.
X1, X2	SK3016 rectifiers.

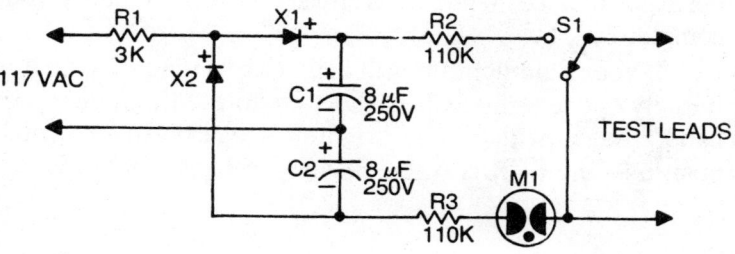

Fig. 58. Capacitor leakage checker circuit.

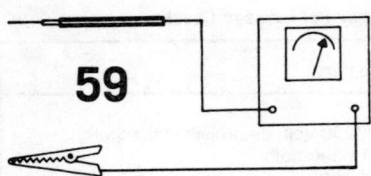

World's Simplest SCR Checker

Believe it or not, most general-purpose SCR's can be checked for good/bad operation--and also for shorted/open condition--with the simple device shown in the accompanying diagram.

With the SCR in question inserted in place of X1, open S1. The bulb should light to approximately half its normal brilliance. When S1 is closed, the light should go out completely.

If your bulb lights to full brilliance when the switch is initially opened, the SCR is short-circuited. If, on the other hand, the bulb does not brighten—regardless of switch position—the SCR is open. See Fig. 59 and Table 59.

Table 59. Parts List for World's Simplest SCR Checker.

Item No.	Description
M1	25-watt household bulb.
R1	6.2k resistor.
S1	Spst switch.
X1	SCR under test.

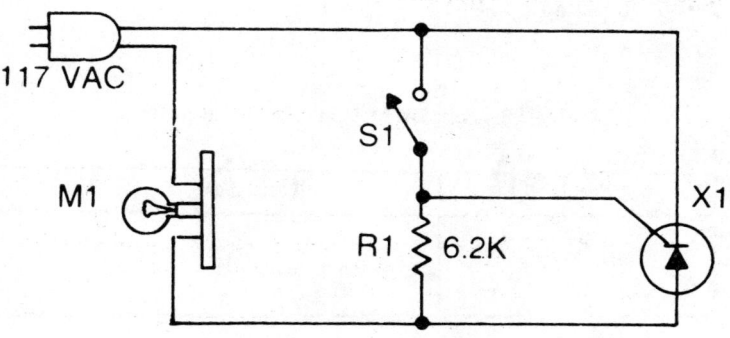

Fig. 59. SCR checker circuit.

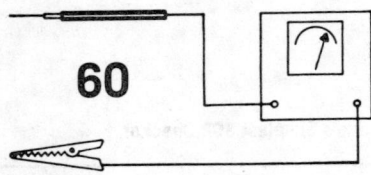

VOM Used To Indicate RF

This set-up is of more use to the ham radio operator than to other electronic experimenters. It provides a visual method of determining that rf is being generated. The small coil, which is made from hook-up wire, can be used in tight spots in the rig.

Set the VOM at the microammeter range or the low milliammeter range. The 1N38B diode will rectify the rf and the result will be indicated on the dial of the VOM. See Fig. 60 and Table 60.

Table 60. Parts List for VOM Used to Indicate RF.

Item No.	Description
L1	4 to 6 turns of insulated wire, wound on ¾-inch diameter rod.
X1	1N38B diode.

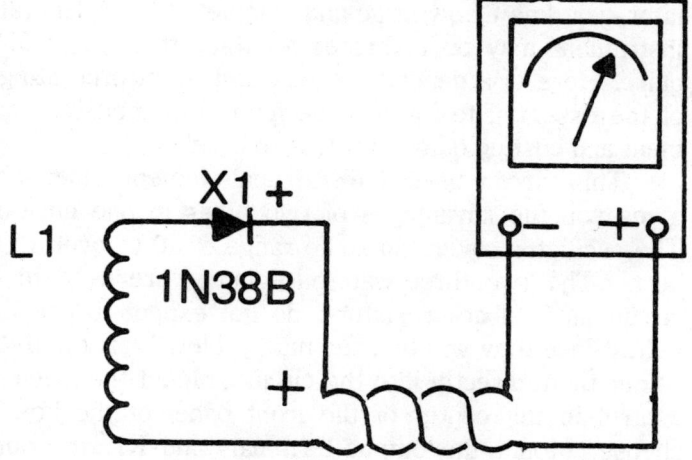

Fig. 60. Rf indicator circuit.

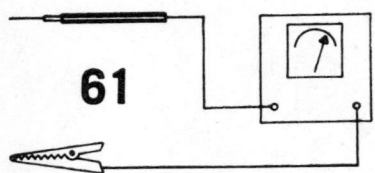

61

Inexpensive 40-13,000 Hertz Audio Oscillator

If you have ever examined a laboratory-type audio oscillator, you know how large and complex it is. A laboratory instrument may be of higher accuracy than you will require. Here is a dependable instrument, incorporating all of the essential features to be found in expensive equipment and costing quite a bit less to build.

This circuit uses a 6EA8 dual-element tube, which gives you the advantages of two tubes in one envelope. The oscillator covers an audio range of 40 to over 13,000 hertz. The two three-watt pilot lamps are used in this circuit as feedback resistors; do not expect to see them light. Since they will be used much below their rated load, solder them directly into the circuit. Mount the frequency control in the center of the front panel of the box you choose. Mount the output terminals and R7, the output attenuator, as you wish, also on the front panel. See Fig. 61 and Table 61.

Calibration will require a frequency meter. Cement a white card to the front of the box around the center of the frequency control R5. Draw a circle of appropriate size. Your calibration marks can be made in pencil and later traced over with India ink. Connect the output terminals of the oscillator directly to the frequency meter. Read the frequency and mark it on the card. Change frequency and repeat until the full range of the oscillator has been calibrated.

Table 61. Parts List for Audio Oscillator.

Item No.	Description
C1	40-40 µF, 250-volt dual section electrolytic capacitor.
C2	.03-µF capacitor.
C3	.47-µF capacitor.
C4	20-µF, 25-volt electrolytic capacitor.
C5	100-µF, 250-volt electrolytic capacitor.
C6	10-µF, 150-volt electrolytic capacitor.
L1	7-H, 50-mA choke (Allied Radio No. 54B1408 or equiv.).
M1,M2	3-watt, 115-volt lamps (Allied Radio No. 60b8834 or equiv.).
R1	75k resistor.
R2	220k resistor.
R3	510-ohm resistor.
R4,R6	11k resistors.
R5	7.5 meg potentiometer.
R7	potentiometer (with switch).
R8	250-ohm resistor.
R9	5100-ohm resistor.
R10	680-ohm resistor.
S1	Part of R7.
T1	Transformer: primary, 117 Vac; secondaries, 125 Vac, 15mA, and 6.3 Vac, 0.6 A (Allied Radio Cat. No. 54B1410 or equiv.).
V1	6EA8 tube1
X1	Rectifier (GE-504A or equiv.).

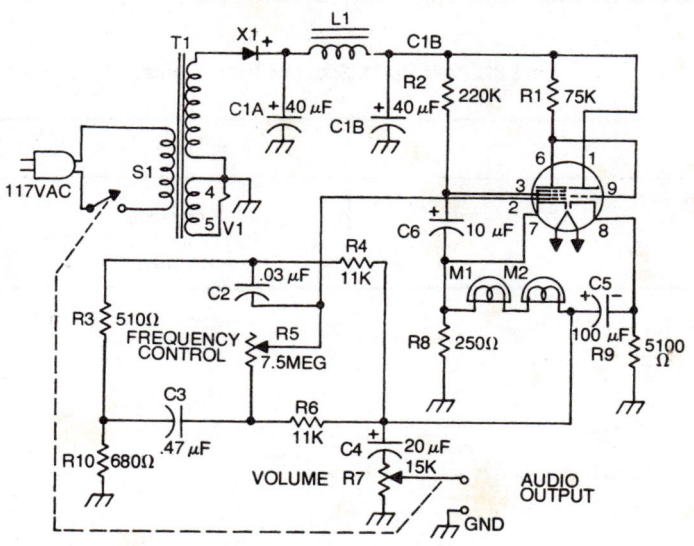

Fig. 61. Audio oscillator circuit.

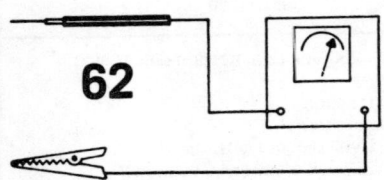

Shop Interference Filter

One of the most annoying things related to radio reception is the interference that is received and that results in noise or buzzing sounds. Much of this interference can be traced to electric razors and vacuum cleaners. If you can locate a source of interference in your home, put a .05 microfarad capacitor across the line. This treatment will usually work.

Some radio interference travels through the air as radio waves. Much of this type of noise enters the home on the 117-volt power line. If this is the problem, construct a filtered cord as indicated (in Fig. 62) for better radio reception. See Fig. 62 and Table 62.

Table 62. Parts List for Shop Interference Filter.

Item No.	Description
C1	.05-μF capacitor. Chassis mount receptacle. 117-volt cord with plug.

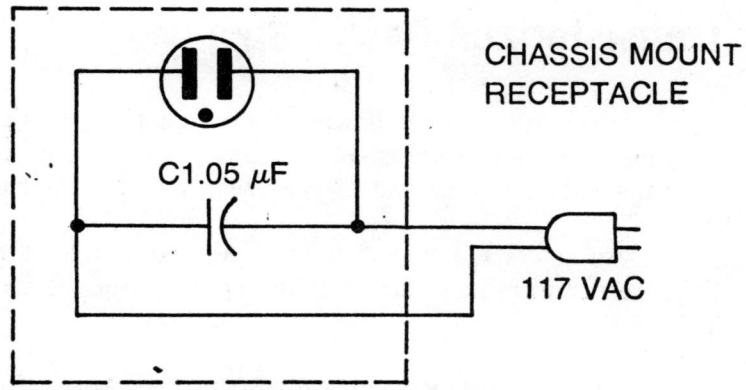

Fig. 62. Interference filter circuit.

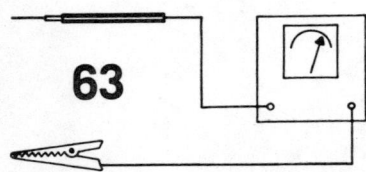

63

Variable Output Transistorized Power Supply

Need a neat little variable power supply to supply voltage for your experimental transistor projects? Try this one. It does not take too much out of your supply of dollars and time.

If you solder the transistor in place, use normal care to protect it from heat due to soldering. See Fig. 63 and Table 63.

Table 63. Parts List for Variable-Output Transistorized Power Supply.

Item No.	Description
C1, C2	35-µF, 15-volt, electrolytic capacitors.
Q1	SK3004 transistor.
R1	7.5k potentiometer.
R2	2k resistor.
R3	0.68-ohm resistor.
T1	Transistor audio transformer (Allied Radio No. 54B2360 or equiv.).
X1	1N60 diode.

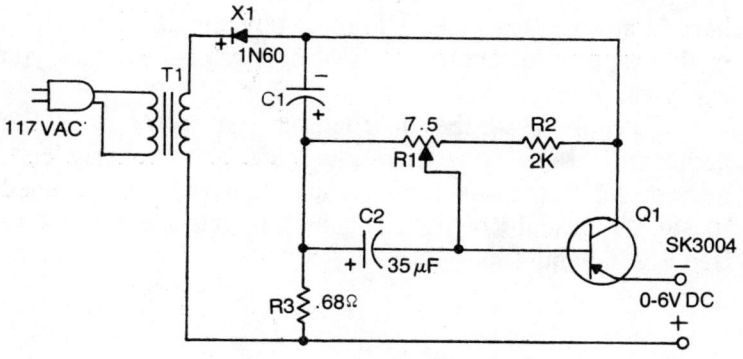

Fig. 63. Variable output power supply circuit.

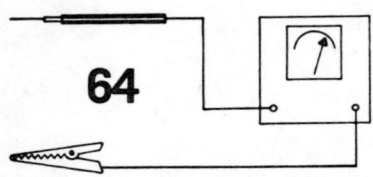

Inexpensive Photo Relay

For those of you who have use for a light-operated relay, here is an excellent one. The most obvious use for a relay of this type is for control of lighting circuits. Perhaps you can think of other uses.

Carefully read the instructions that come with the photo cell. Make sure that the leads are properly connected. R1 is the sensitivity adjustment and will be used to set the amount of light required to operate the relay. See Fig. 64 and Table 64.

Table 64. Parts List for Inexpensive Photo Relay.

Item No.	Description
C1	25-μF, 25-volt, electrolytic capacitor.
K1	Relay (Advance Type 50/1C/4000D or equiv.).
B1	7.5-volt battery.
B2	1.5-volt battery.
M1	Photo cell (Solar Systems Type 10-6L or equiv.).
Q1	2N228 transistor.
Q2	SK3004 transistor.
R1	1meg potentiometer.
R2	100-ohm resistor.
R3	4.7k resistor.
S1	Spst switch.

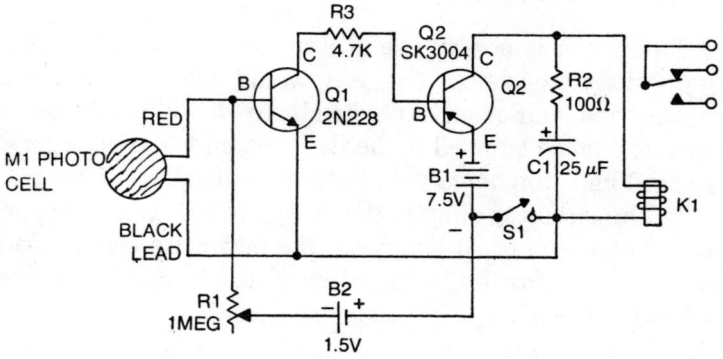

Fig. 64. Photo relay circuit.

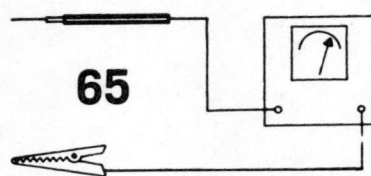

Footswitch Unit Controller

A footswitch is a very useful item to own. You can use a footswitch anywhere that you would like to control ac power and you need both hands to do other things. A footswitch can be used in the dark room for the enlarger or to start and stop home workshop machinery.

The circuit is simple, the complete unit can be housed in a metal box, or, if you wish, the enclosure can be made of some composition material such as *Masonite*. See Fig. 65 and Table 65.

Table 65. Parts List for Footstitch Unit Controller.

Item No.	Description
M1, M2	Flush power receptacles.
S1	Spst switch, 10A capacity (Allied Radio No. 56B5328 or equiv.).

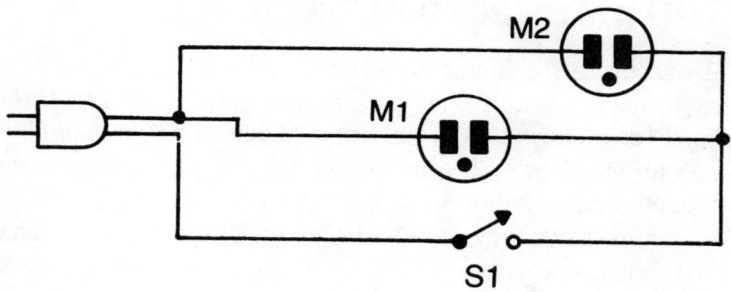

Fig. 65. Footswitch unit-controller circuit.

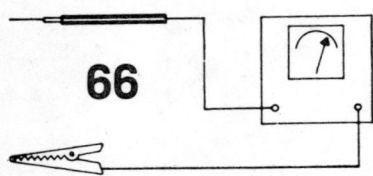

100 kHz Receiver Calibrator

An accurate frequency standard is very useful to the ham radio man; without one, he may not dare to approach the band edge. The FCC is very strict about out-of-band operation. The SWL may be doubtful of the station being received if he cannot be sure of its frequency.

This frequency standard will generate a small signal that will appear every 100 kHz or 1/10 MHz on your receiver.

Construction is quite simple and straight forward. Check the various tube pin terminals for resistance after construction. If you have an error it will show up. Connect the output lead to the antenna terminal of your receiver, warm up the calibrator and set the capacitor C1 for "zero beat" (inaudible signal) and you are all set. See Fig. 66 and Table 66.

Table 66. Parts List for 100 KHz Receiver Calibrator.

Item No.	Description
C1	3-32-pF miniature variable capacitor (Allied Radio No. 43B3766 or equiv.).
C2, C5	.01-µF capacitors.
C3	5-pF disc ceramic capacitor.
C4	220-pF capacitor.
C6	50-µF, 150-volt, electrolytic capacitor.
R1	620-ohm resistor.
R2	1.1k resistor.
R3	110k resistor.
R4	220k resistor.
R5	100-ohm, 2-watt resistor.
T1	Power transformer: primary 117 Vac, secondary 117 Vac at 15mA, 6.3 Vac at 0.6A (Allied Radio No. 54B3710 or equiv.).
V1	6AU6 tube.
X1	Rectifier (GE-504A or equiv.).
	100 kHz crystal.

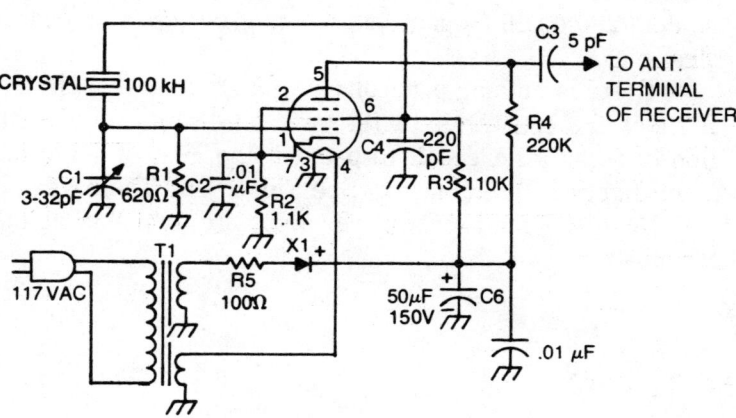

Fig. 66. Receiver calibrator circuit.

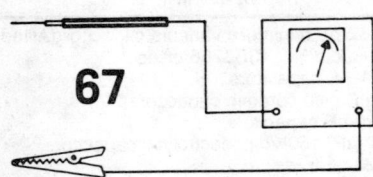

High-Frequency Oscillator

A crystal oscillator is a very much needed and much desired adjunct to any collection of test instruments. It serves as a frequency standard from which other instruments, receivers, etc. can be calibrated. A crystal oscillator is useful at other than the crystal frequency. Its harmonics can be detected at lower strength than the fundamental. For instance, a 10-megacycle oscillator can be detected on 10 megacycles, 20 megacycles, 40 megacycles, etc.

There is nothing particularly touchy about this circuit. It should be constructed with care, observing the precaution of using a heat sink to prevent the heat of soldering from affecting the transistor. See Fig. 67 and Table 67.

Up to 10 milliwatts of rf output are available at the terminals.

Table 67. Parts List for High-Frequency Oscillator.

Item No.	Description
C1, C3, C4	.005-μF capacitors.
C2	See L2.
L1	2.5-mH choke (National R-50 or equiv.).
L2	This value to be chosen with C2 to resonate at the crystal frequency.
L3	2 to 3 turns of wire wrapped about the lower end of L2.
B1	7.5-volt battery.
Q1	SK3011 transistor.
R1	110-ohm resistor.
R2	20k resistor.
R3	390-ohm resistor.
S1	Spst switch.
	Crystal.

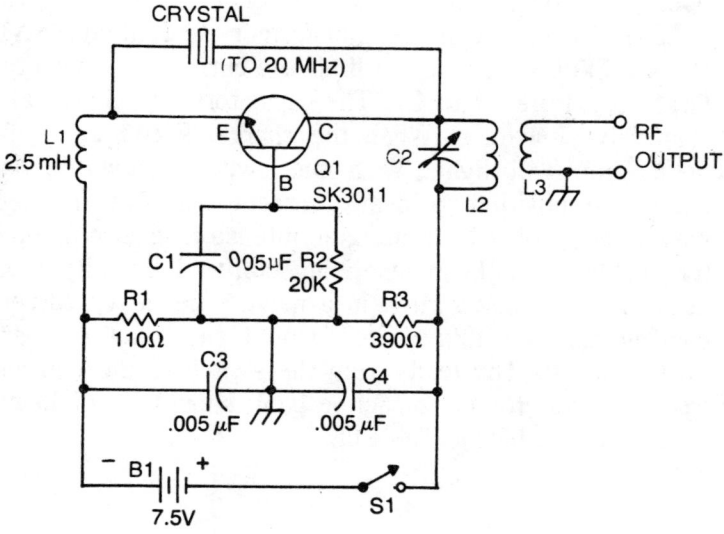

Fig. 67. High-frequency oscillator circuit.

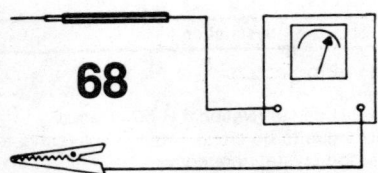

Automatic Tool Magnetizer

The home craftsman will have many uses for a tool magnetizer. How about all those times you have lost a nut or other part and have wished for a magnetized tool? Here is the way to make your own magnetizer.

A look at the circuit will explain how this magnetizer operates. For safety, a transformer is included in the circuit. The output of the transformer is rectified by X1. R1 is a limiting resistor to limit the current flow into the large capacitors C1 to C5. The capacitors will charge at a relatively slow rate. When the charge is complete, the neon lamp will light. With the switch thrown in the magnetize position, a heavy current will flow through magnetizing coil L1, creating an intense magnetic field. A tool inserted in the magnetizing coil will be fully magnetized. The knife switch is a must. The heavy current passing through this switch would cause an ordinary switch to fail. The leads from the switch to the coil and from the coil to the capacitor bank should be of heavy wire. See Fig. 68 and Table 68.

Table 68. Parts List for Automatic Tool Magnetizer.

Item No.	Description
C1 thru C5	200-μF, 150-volt, electrolytic capacitors, connected in parallel.
F1	1-A fuse.
L1	Magnetizing coil, 8 turns No. 10 wire, ¾-inch diameter, ⅛-inch space between turns.
M1	NE-2E neon lamp.
R1	100k 10-watt resistor (wirewound).
R2	120k resistor.
R3	130k resistor.
S1	Spst switch.
S2	Dpdt knife switch.
T1	Transformer: primary 117 Vac, secondary 117 volts @ 50 A (Allied Radio No. 54B1411 or equiv.).
X1	Rectifier (GE-504A or equiv.).

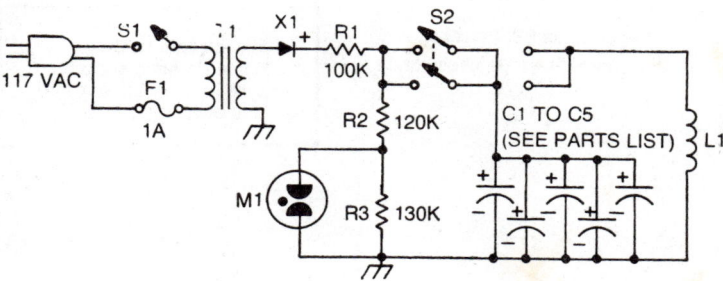

Fig. 68. Tool magnetizer circuit.

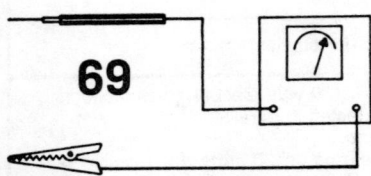

Handy Vibrator Rejuvenator

This is a method that can be used to put a troublesome vibrator back in condition. Most vibrators must be replaced because the contacts stick together and the vibrator will not "start."

A few minutes of this treatment are usually sufficient to put your vibrator back in operating condition. See Fig. 69 and Table 69.

Table 69. Parts List for Vibrator Rejuvenator.	Description
	50-watt light bulb. Porcelain lamp socket. 2 insulated alligator clips. Line cord.

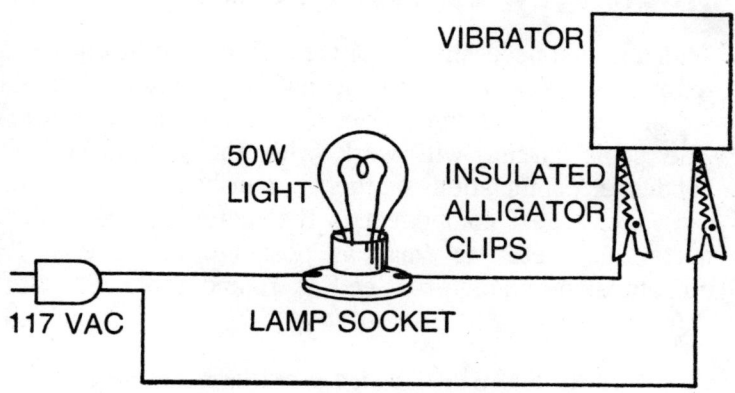

Fig. 69. Vibrator rejuvenator circuit.

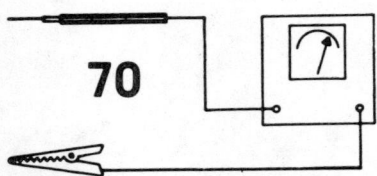

Diode-Type CB Field Strength Meter

This unit is a necessity for Citizens Band operators. Use it to improve transmitter tuning and to monitor on-the-air signal strength. L1 and C1 are chosen for CB frequencies. The same circuit will work with the necessary coil/condenser combinations on the amateur bands.

The largest component is the meter. If you wish to make this meter as small as possible, use one of the miniature milliammeters. See Fig. 70 and Table 70.

Table 70. Parts List for Diode-Type CB Field Strength Meter.

Item No.	Description
C1	Antenna, 36" whip.
	15-130-pF padder capacitor (Allied Radio No. 17U093 or equiv.).
C2	.005-μF capacitor.
L1	20 turns No. 24 wire, ⅝-inch diameter coil, tapped as shown.
M1	0-1 milliammeter.
X1	1N34A diode.

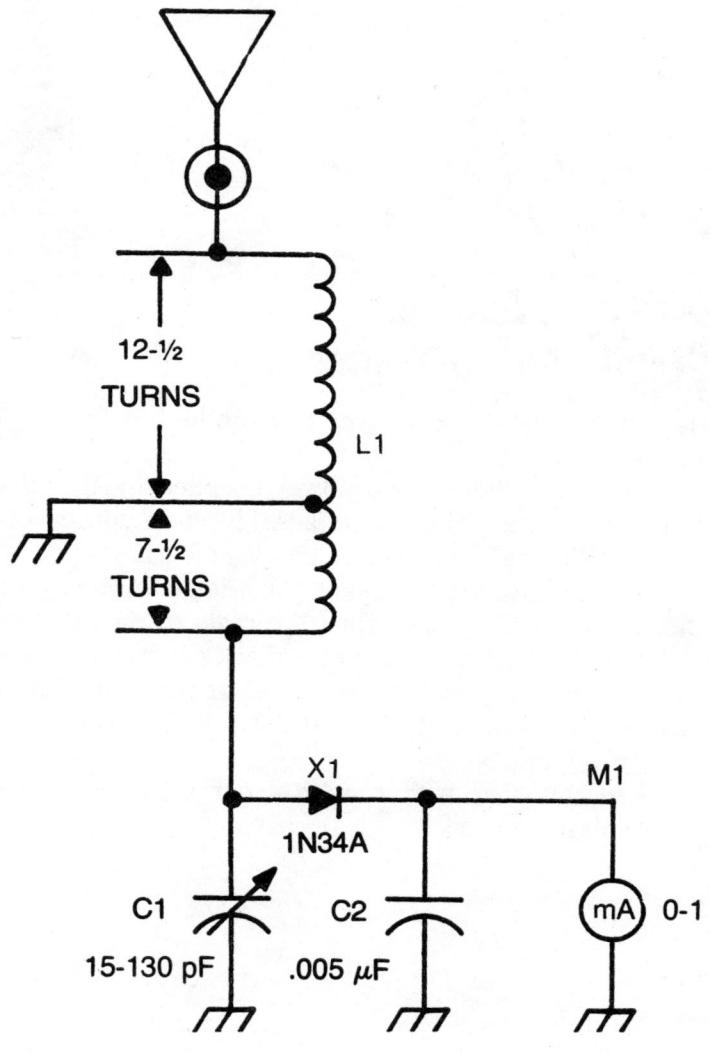

Fig. 70. Field strength meter circuit.

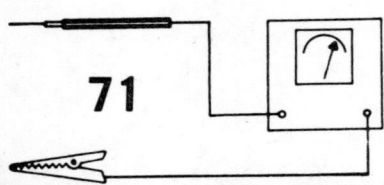

Simple Audio Tracer

Here is a simple signal tracer that can be "cooked-up" in an hour or so.

Note that there is no power supplied by this troubleshooting tool. That is because it does not inject a signal; it "listens" to signals in the defective unit.

To use it, connect crystal or high-impedance magnetic phones to the terminals. Tune the radio to the strongest local station. Unlike the use of a signal generator, start at the antenna and listen to the signal at grid and plate of each tube until the signal is lost. That is the faulty stage. See Fig. 71 and Table 71.

Use this unit with caution—your ears can receive quite a blast of sound.

Table 71. Parts List for Simple Audio Tracer.

Item No.	Description
C1, C2 S1 X1	.01-μF capacitors. Spst switch. 1N118 diode. 2 alligator clips. 2 jacks to accept your earphones.

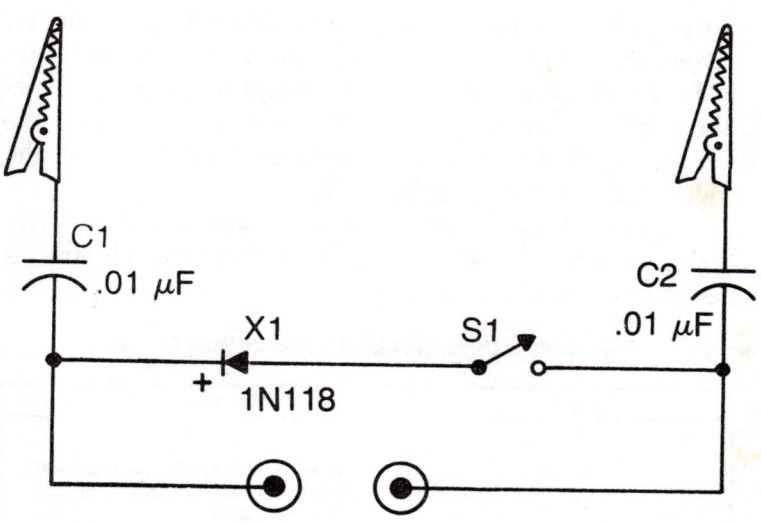

Fig. 71. Audio tracer circuit.

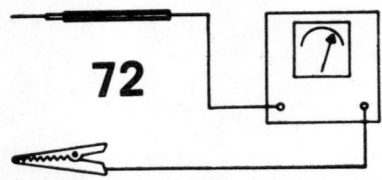

Transistorized Square-Wave Generator

A square-wave generator is a very worthwhile item of test equipment for checking the linearity of amplifiers. Most of us would like to own one but do not have the money. Here is one you can build that will not be too expensive.

Construct this unit in any convenient enclosure, with the shaft of S1 projecting through the front. All components can be wired in place, with the exception of R4. Instead, wire a 1-megohm potentiometer in place of R4. Insert the battery and connect to the vertical input terminals of your scope. Vary the resistance of the potentiometer until the square waves are symmetrical. Check the resistance at the best setting and use this figure as the value of R4. See Fig. 72 and Table 72.

To use the generator, connect as shown in the sketch. Refer to your scope instructions for information on interpretation of scope patterns.

Table 72. Parts List for Transistorized Square-Wave Generator.

Item No.	Description
C1	10-μF, 6-volt, electrolytic capacitor.
C2	50 μF, 6-volt, electrolytic capacitor.
C3	.02-μF capacitor.
C4	.002-μF capacitor.
C5	200-pF capacitor.
B1	1.5-volt battery.
M1	RCA phone jack.
Q1, Q2	SK3011 transistors.
R1	2.2k resistor.
R2	110k resistor.
R3	620-ohm resistor.
R4	620k resistor.
S1	2-pole 4-position switch.

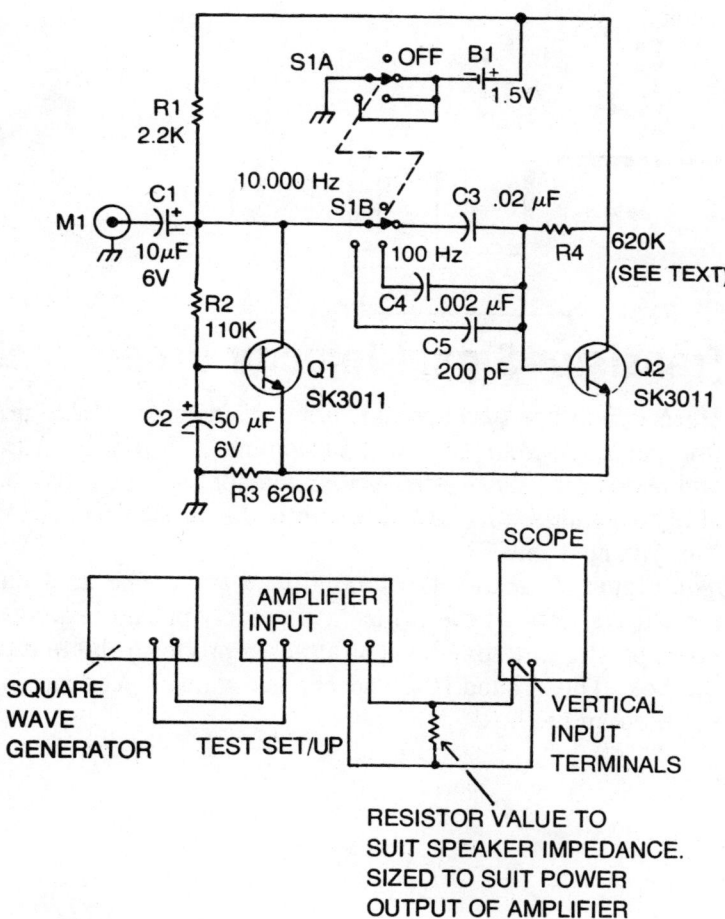

Fig. 72. Square-wave generator circuit.

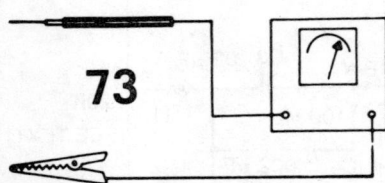

Transistor Signal-Injector Probe

Here is another excellent little signal injector. There are few parts, so your cost will be minimal. If you use care and choose the smallest possible components, you may be able to include all these parts into the probe itself. See Fig. 73 and Table 73.

Figure 73 shows the ground lead and probe as separate. If you can get the components nicely placed in a good sized plastic pill box or such, attach a probe to the end of the box. The ground lead and clip are a must. You cannot put them in the box.

Table 73. Parts List for Transistor Signal-Injector Probe.

Item No.	Description
C1	.005-µF capacitor.
C2	.01-µF capacitor.
B1	15-volt battery.
Q1	2N109 transistor.
R1	510k resistor.
R2	1.5meg potentiometer with switch S1 included.
S1	Part of 1.5meg potentiometer.
T1	Transistor output transformer: 825-ohm primary, 16-ohm secondary. (Allied Radio No. 54B2360 or equiv.).

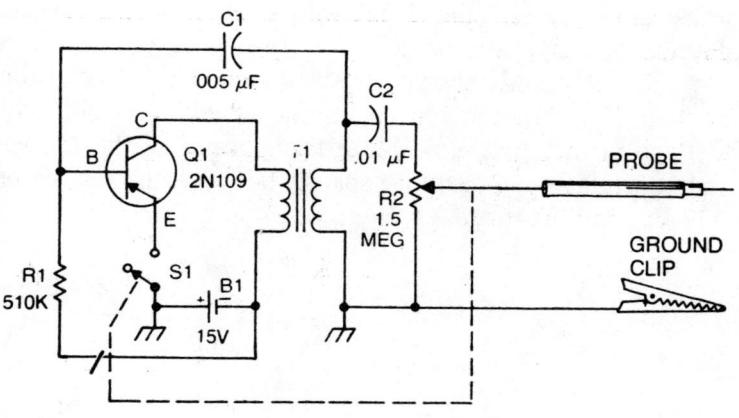

Fig. 73. Signal-injector probe circuit.

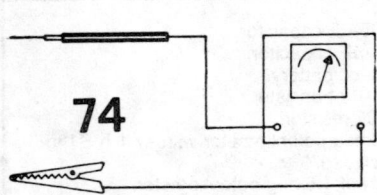

DC Motor Supply Unit

Many dc motors are available on the surplus market at reasonable prices. Sometimes we pass over a real bargain because it happens to be dc.

The schematic shown here will supply 117 Vdc at the socket. If the motor you choose is meant for a different voltage do not give up. Use a transformer of the proper output voltage and current capacity between the source of 117 Vac and the diode X1. See Fig. 74 and Table 74.

Table 74. Parts List for DC Motor Supply Unit.

Item No.	Description
C1	80-μF, 150-volt electrolytic capacitor.
M1	Plug-in type receptacle.
X1	Rectifier (GE-504A or equiv.).

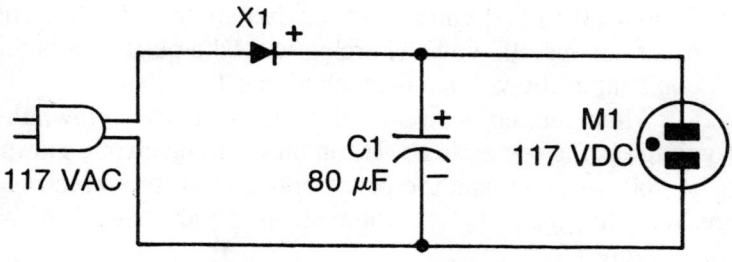

Fig. 74. Dc motor supply circuit.

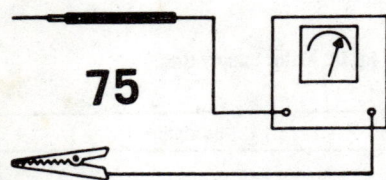

Neon-Lamp Polarity Tester

A simple polarity tester can be made from a neon lamp, a resistor, and a set of test prods. It will work for voltages of about 80 to 500 volts. Use another method of checking polarity above 500 volts as arcing will take place inside the neon lamp if the voltage is much higher than that.

When testing a circuit, if both electrodes glow, the voltage being tested is ac. When only one electrode glows, the voltage is dc, and the prod connected to that electrode is touching the negative point of the circuit. See Fig. 75 and Table 75.

Table 75. Parts List for Neon-Lamp Polarity Tester.

Item No.	Description
M1	NE-51 neon lamp.
R1	200k resistor.
	1 set of test prods.

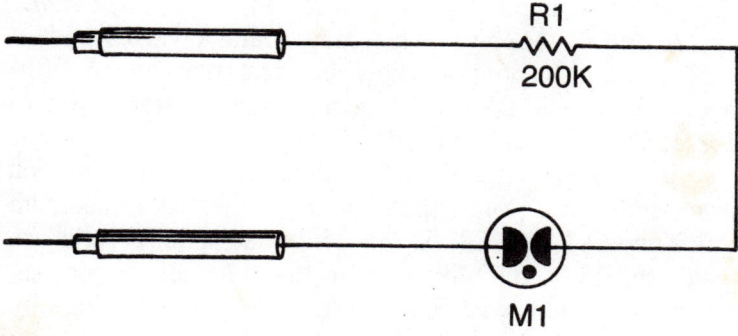

Fig. 75. Polarity tester circuit.

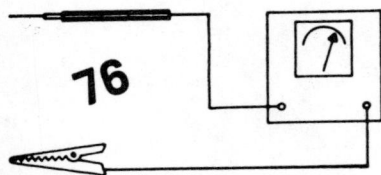

108 MHz Receiver Calibrator

A truly unusual item designed for the technician who is handy with vhf construction and who needs a reliable reference oscillator with 108 MHz output, the circuit shown in the accompanying diagram can produce a healthy 25 milliwatts of signal—and is capable of generating even more, depending on individual oscillator operational efficiency and loading constants.

As with any vhf project, *leads should be kept short, direct, and to-the-point.* This may seem a verbal redundancy, but it cannot possibly be overstressed. A fifth-overtone type M-20 crystal or a similar crystal keyed to 108 MHz output can be used.

In operation, L2 should be adjusted to just a fraction past oscillator kick-in—then trimmed later from maximum efficiency. L1 and L3, if the Miller adjustable coils are used, should be initially set with the slugs all the way in, trimming output with C7. L1/L3 can be optimized by slight tuning later, although rough inductance of 2.6 μh should do the trick. Final balancing of C2 (optimum performance should be at 5-6 pF) and C7 should put this gadget in fine working order. See Fig. 76 and Table 76.

Table 76. Parts List for 108 MHz Receiver Calibrator.

Item No.	Description
C1	120-pF capacitor.
C2, C7	8-pF variable capacitors.
C3	500-pF capacitor.
C4	40-pF variable capacitor.
C5	20-pF capacitor.
C6	.002-µF capacitor.
L1, L4	Homemade coils, approx. 2.6 µh. Or use J. W. Miller 4503 slug-tuned variables or equivalent.
L2	Coil (J. W. Miller 4302 or equivalent).
L3	Homemade coil, wound with three turns of No. 21 wire, spacewound on ¼-in diameter coil form.
B1	1.5-volt battery.
B2	24-volt battery.
M3	Fifth-overtone, 108-MHz crystal (McCoy Type M-20, or equivalent).
Q1	HEP-2 transistor.
R1	160-ohm resistor.
S1	Spst switch.

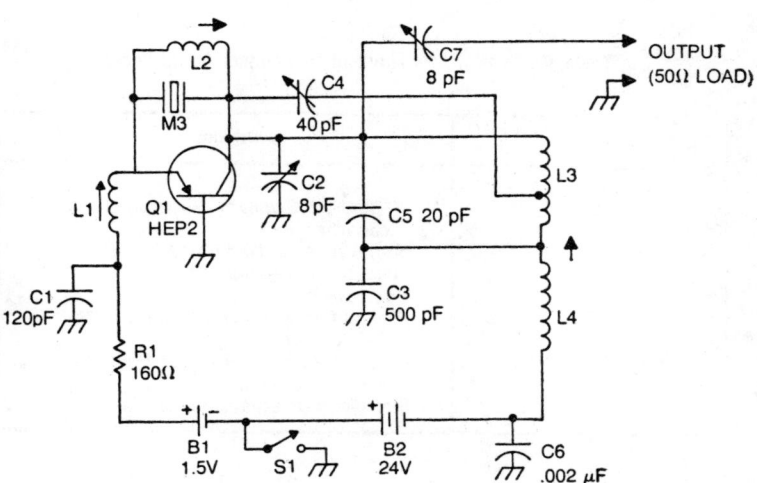

Fig. 76. 108 MHz receiver calibrator circuit.

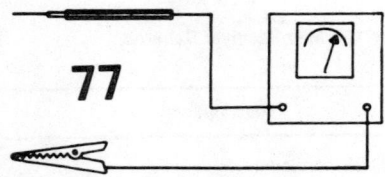

Filament Transformer Power Supply

There is always a need for a power supply when working with test gear. Here is one you can make using those spare filament transformers you have on hand. Catalog numbers are furnished in case the transformers are not already at hand.

This circuit takes advantage of a "back-to-back" arrangement of the filament transformers to provide 120 volts dc as well as 6.3 volts ac, with isolation from the power line. See Fig. 77 and Table 77.

None of the component specifications are critical.

Table 77. Parts List for Filament Transformer Power Supply.

Item No	Description
C1	30-30μF, 250-volt, dual-section electrolytic capacitor.
L1	50-mA choke (Allied Radio No. 54B1407).
R1	30k, 10-watt resistor.
S1	Spst switch.
T1	Filament transformer (Allied Radio No. 54B2031 or equiv.).
T2	Filament transformer (Allied Radio No. 54B1419 or equiv.).
X1	8D4 diode (International Rectifier).

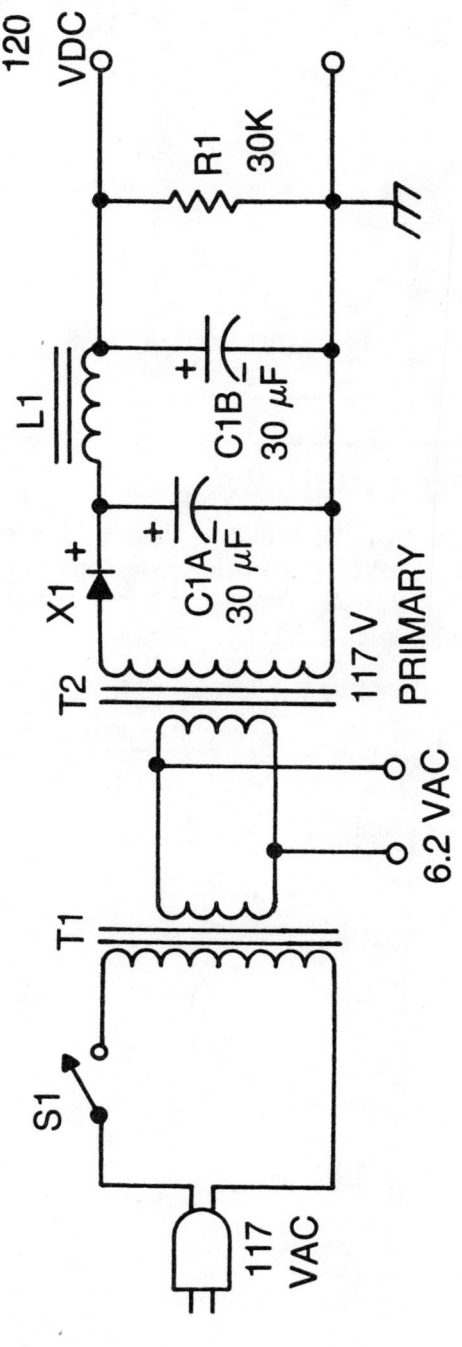

Fig. 77. Filament transformer power supply circuit.

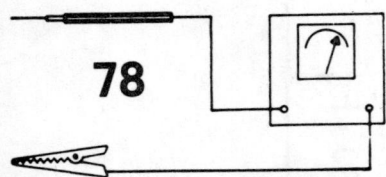

Blown Fuse Indicator

This refinement can be added to almost any piece of gear with little difficulty. Connect the neon lamp in series with the proper resistor and connect the two across the fuse. Should the fuse open, the lamp will glow.

$$\text{The resistance of R1} = \frac{\text{voltage across the fuse}}{.0025}$$

See Fig. 78 and Table 78.

Table 78. Parts List for Blown Fuse Indicator.

Item No.	Description
M1 R1	NE-2 neon lamp. (See Text).

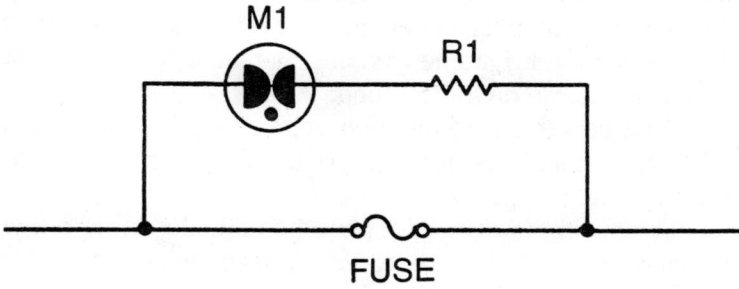

Fig. 78. Blown fuse indicator circuit.

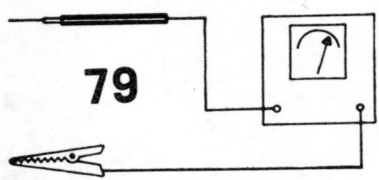

TV Picture Tube Rejuvenator

The picture your TV set produces gradually becomes grayer and has less and less contrast until at last something must be done. This usually means that oxide deposits have built up on the cathode exterior so that electrons cannot escape to do their job.

Sometimes these oxides can be burned away to provide some improvement in picture quality. If, however, the picture tube has been previously rejuvenated or if there is a tube brightener already installed, there may not be much you can do for the tube.

The center tap of the high-voltage winding of the old TV transformer used for this project is cut short and the exposed end is taped to insulate it.

In use, the switch S1 should be held closed for a few seconds at a time. Use repeated applications of voltage for best results. See Fig. 79 and Table 79.

Table 79. Parts List for TV Picture Tube Rejuvenator.

Item No.	Description
C1, C2	30-μF, 450-volt electrolytic capacitors.
R1	300-ohm, 10-watt resistor.
R2	1meg, 2-watt resistor.
S1	Spst switch.
T1	Transformer (see text) or (Allied Radio No. 54B1429 or equiv.).
V1	5R4 tube.
	1 picture tube socket with leads.

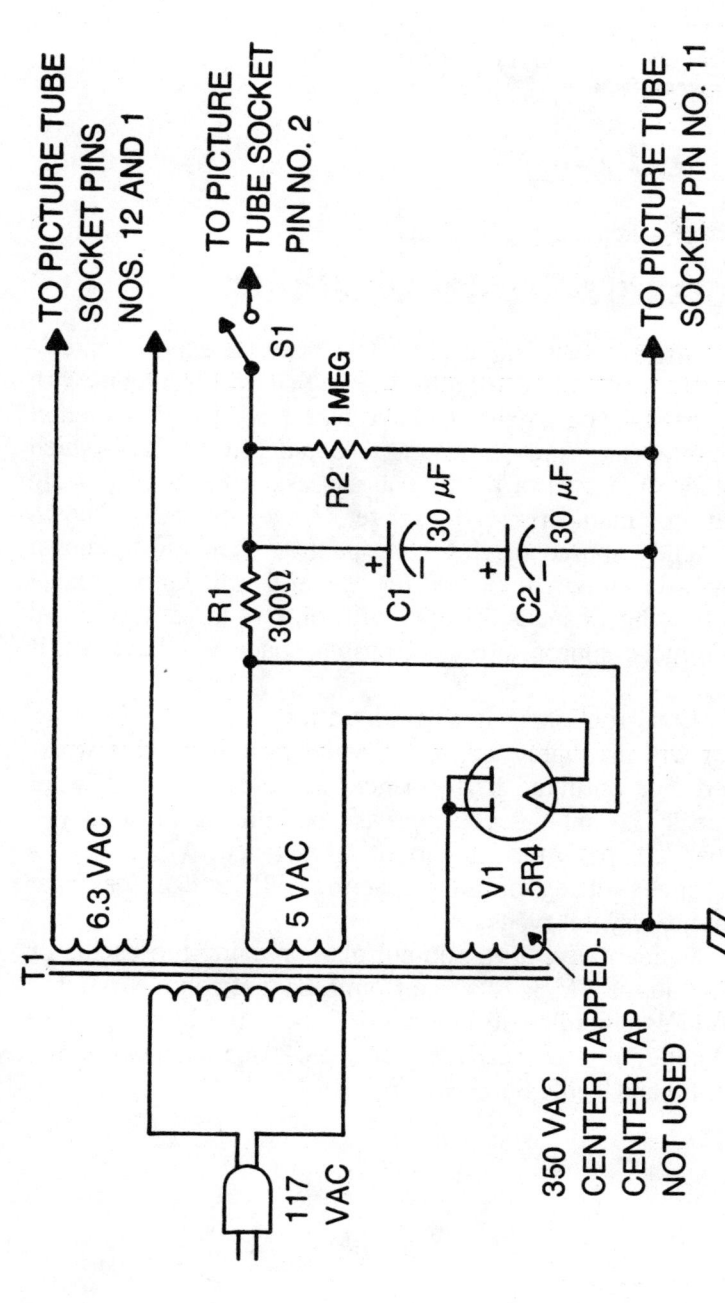

Fig. 79. Picture tube rejuvenator circuit.

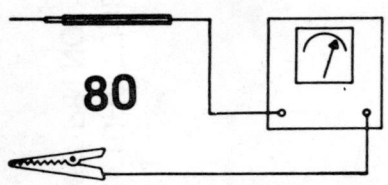

80

Versatile Crystal Oscillator

This little easy-to-build gadget is truly an experimenter's delight: a reliable crystal oscillator that will "trigger" with any crystal you happen to have handy with a fundamental frequency anywhere between 1.75 and 14.00 MHz—which includes most all of them! You can use it for bandspotting your communications or amateur receiver, as a known frequency source driving a scope (for checking unknown generator frequency), or for general television troubleshooting. Chances are you will think of at least a dozen even more appropriate applications once you have got it going.

Construction is not at all critical. In fact, the oscillator will invariably kick in without any adjustments whatever! For optimum performance, however, you will want to peak C1 and—as you increase operational frequency—adjust L1 for more in-circuit inductance. Generally, a midrange setting of the capacitor will suffice for most common crystal types.

Incidentally, if you do not plan on using the oscillator much above 7MHz, you can omit L1 entirely. Note: the 2N247's "shield" lead is used; it is situated between base and collector (two leads left of red dot) on transistor. See Fig. 80 and Table 80.

Table 80. Parts List for Versatile Crystal Oscillator.

Item No.	Description
C1	30-pF variable capacitor.
C2	50-pF capacitor.
C3	800-pF capacitor.
C4	.005 µF.
L1	Coil (J. W. Miller 4503 or equiv.).
B1	6-volt battery.
M2	Any fundamental frequency crystal in 1.75 through 14.00 MHz range.
Q1	2N247 transistor.
R1	120k resistor.
R2	1.1k resistor.
S1	Spst switch.

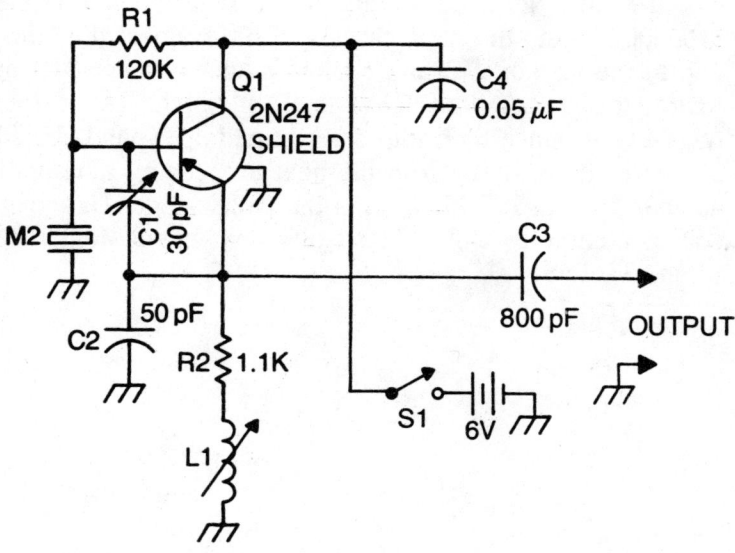

Fig. 80. Versatile crystal oscillator circuit.

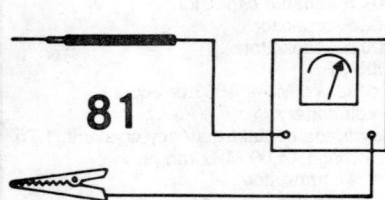

Two-Transistor Signal Generator

One of the most useful pieces of test equipment you can own is the signal generator. This signal generator can be used to troubleshoot most electronic gear.

To find the faulty stage in a radio, connect the grounded clip to the radio chassis. Next, connect the other clip to the grid of the radio's audio output tube. Set R1 at midrange and R2 full on. R1 controls the pitch. R2 controls the volume. Once the radio has warmed up, sound should be heard. If so, proceed to the next proceeding tube until no sound is heard. This then is the faulty stage. Use your volt-ohmmeter to isolate the faulty component. See Fig. 81 and Table 81.

Table 81. Parts List for Two-Transistor Signal Generator.

Item No.	Description
C1	.001-μF capacitor.
C2	.02-μF capacitor.
B1	9-volt battery.
Q1	SK7 transistor.
Q2	SK3004 transistor.
R1	1meg potentiometer.
R2	1k potentiometer.
R3	51k resistor.
	2 alligator clips.
	Length of shielded cable.

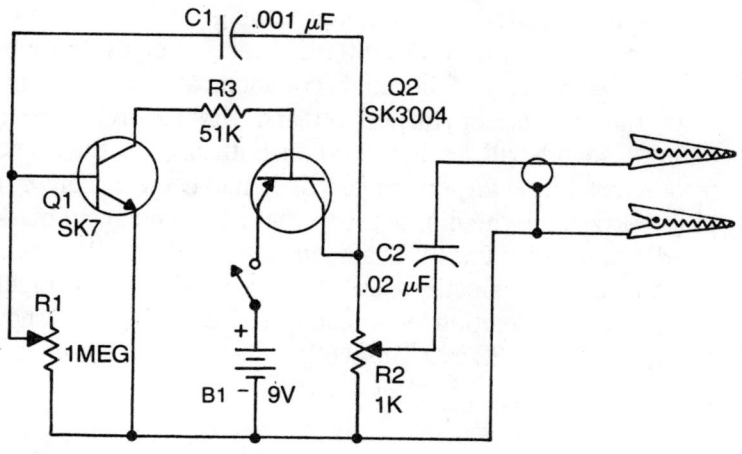

Fig. 81. Signal generator circuit.

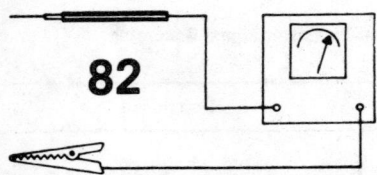

One-Transistor Dip Meter

The ham or CB enthusiast should not be without a reliable dip meter. With this meter, it will not be necessary to guess at coil/capacitor combinations; just connect them as they would be in the circuit in question and "dip" them with this unit.

A dip meter is a variable oscillator. When the probe of this variable oscillator is held close to a tuned circuit, the tuned circuit will absorb some of the rf energy generated. As the variable oscillator (dip meter) is tuned to the same frequency as the tuned circuit, a pronounced dip is noticed as indicated by the meter reading.

The range is from 5 to 60 megahertz. For calibration, use an accurately calibrated communications receiver. With the dip meter turned on and the receiver on, a definite sound will be heard when both are on the same frequency. Mark the dip meter dial, move the receiver 1 megahertz, tune the dip meter to that point and again mark the dip meter dial until it has been calibrated for all scales.

Make all connections as rigid as possible as a slight change in the position of a lead could cause a frequency change. See Fig. 82 and Table 82.

Table 82. Parts List for One-Transistor Dip Meter.

Item No.	Description
C1, C2	.015-μF capacitors.
C3, C5	15-pF disc ceramic capacitors.
C4	50-pF variable capacitor. (E. F. Johnson No. 148-4 or equiv.).
L1	38 turns Air Dux 532T coil stock tapped at 15, 23, 30, 34, and 38 turns.
L2	See enlarged detail.
B1	13.5-volt battery.
M1, M2	Phone tip jacks.
M4	0-50 microammeter.
Q1	SK3007 transistor.
R1	35k potentiometer.
R2	1.1k resistor.
R3	3.6k resistor.
R4	36k resistor.
S1	Dpst switch.
S2	Single pole, six-position nonshorting switch.
X1	1N38B diode.

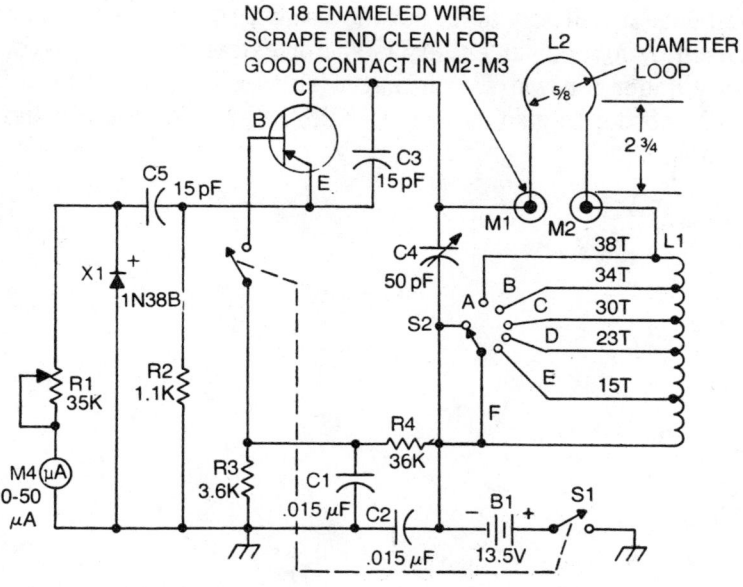

Fig. 82. Dip meter circuit.

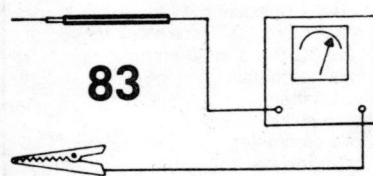

RF Meter

An rf meter can be useful to the ham radio or CB operator. Just tune the multiplier and final stages for maximum meter reading, always keeping in mind that the maximum rating of the rig should not be exceeded.

This simple and useful tool is easily made and as easy to use. It will handle all but the largest rigs and yet can be used by low power enthusiasts. For extremely low power, say under ten watts, you may wish to reduce the value of R3 in order to gain more meter deflection. See Fig. 83 and Table 83.

Table 83. Parts List for An RF Meter.

Item No.	Description
C1, C2	.0047-μF, 500-volt capacitors.
M1, M2	antenna fittings.
M3	0-1 milliammeter.
R1	6k, 5-watt resistor.
R2	2.5k, 2-watt potentiometer.
R3	9100-ohm, 1-watt resistor.
X1	1N38B diode.

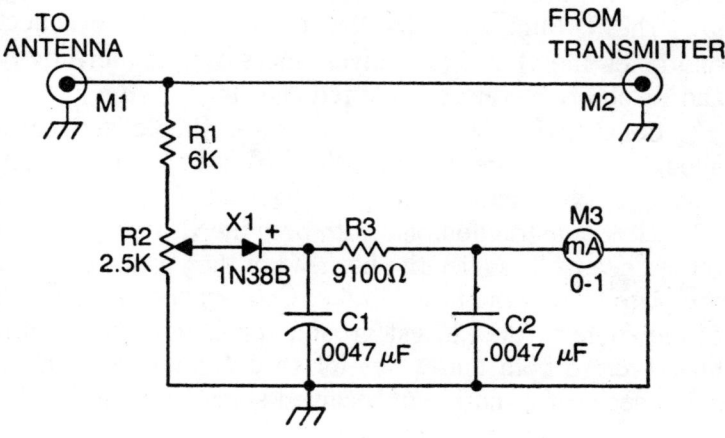

Fig. 83. Rf voltmeter circuit.

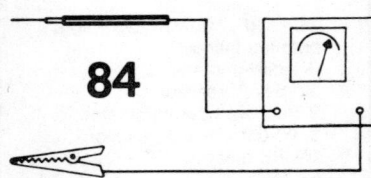

One-Tube CB Q-Multiplier

A good Q-multiplier can make your sad-acting ham radio receiver sound and act like a much more expensive rig. It does this by operating on the receiver's intermediate frequency. This particular one was designed for use with receivers having a 455 kHz i-f. It will not work on other frequencies without modification.

The Q-Multiplier, as the name implies, in effect multiplies the Q of the receiver, increasing its selectivity and its ability to reject unwanted signals.

Construction of this unit is quite simple and parts should cost no more than $15.00. Cost can be considerably less if you have some of the parts on hand.

After construction, and with both the Q-Multiplier and the receiver off, solder the hot lead of the coaxial cable to the plate lead of the first i-f tube. Connect the ground side of the cable to the closest ground connection. Now, turn on power to both units. Set R4 to maximum resistance. Now, set R4 for maximum received signal without oscillation. See Fig. 84 and Table 84.

To align the Q-Multiplier, set R4 to minimum resistance setting; adjust L1 until a loud whistling sound is heard from the speaker. Now, reset R4 to a higher resistance. Experimentation with the adjustment of R4 will indicate the best results.

Table 84. Parts List for One-Tube CB Q-Multiplier.

Item No.	Description
C1	.005-μF, disc ceramic capacitor.
C2	620-pF capacitor.
C3	.0025-μF capacitor.
C4	500-pF capacitor.
C5	50-50 μF, 150-volt dual-section electrolytic capacitor.
L1	Loopstick (J. W. Miller 2007 or equiv.).
R1	11k resistor.
R2	2meg resistor.
R3	2k resistor.
R4	7.5k potentiometer.
R5	4.3k, 1-watt resistor.
T1	Power transformer: primary, 117 Vac; secondaries, 125 Vac at 15mA and 6.3 Vac at .6 A (Allied Radio No. 54B1410 or equiv.).
V1	6100 tube.
X1	Rectifier (GE-504A or equiv.).

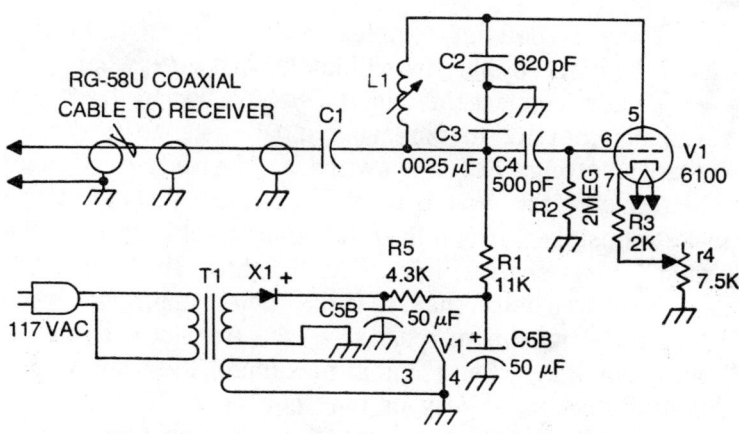

Fig. 84. CB Q-multimeter circuit.

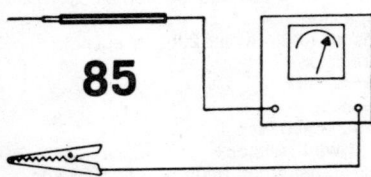

In-Circuit Transistor Tester

A transistor tester is much in demand these days and one that can be used without removing the questionable transistor is a real boon. Here is one you can build for a few dollars.

There is nothing complex here, so build it to suit. Label the clips so that you will know what goes where.

To use, connect the clips to the appropriate transistor terminals. Set R2 to the maximum resistance (low base current) setting. Set the switch as desired to NPN or PNP. (Note: the transistor will not be damaged if you make a mistake.) If you have the switch set correctly, the "good" lamp should light. The brighter the light, the better the transistor quality. If the "bad" lamp lights when R2 is set at maximum resistance, the transistor is bad. If both lamps light when R2 is at maximum, the transistor is doubtful, that is, it may or may not work. Reduced settings of R2 give higher base currents for testing less sensitive transistors. However R2 should not be reduced to minimum or a "bad" indication may be obtained, regardless of the condition of the transistor being tested. See Fig. 85 and Table 85.

Table 85. Parts List for In-Circuit Transistor Tester.

Item No.	Description
C1	.1-μF capacitor.
C2	.05-μF capacitor.
B1	2 1.5-volt batteries in series.
M1	NE-51 neon lamp.
M2	2-volt incandescent lamp (GE No. 49 or equiv.).
R1	210-ohm resistor.
R2	15k potentiometer.
S1	2-pole, 3-position switch.
T1	Audio transformer, 1.5k-ohm ct primary, 500k-ohm secondary (Argonne AR-141 or equiv.).

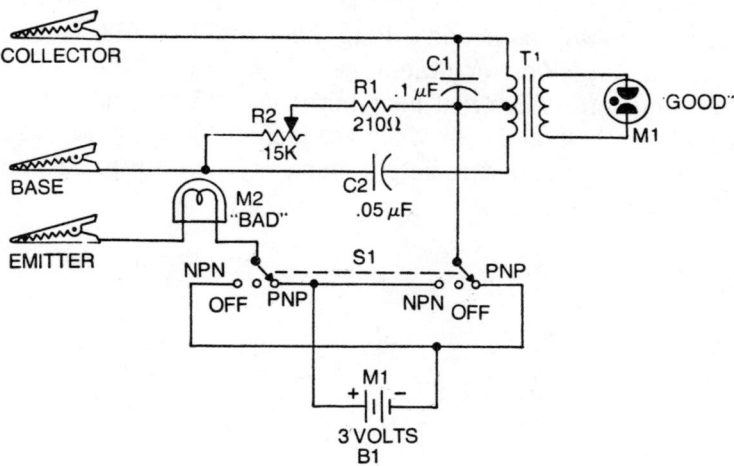

Fig. 85. In-circuit transistor tester circuit.

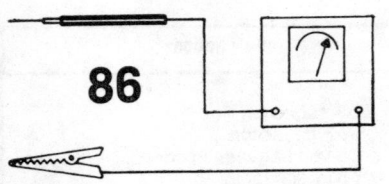

Radiation Finder

Do you want to go prospecting for uranium? The item that stops some of us is the cost of the Geiger counter radiation detector that is necessary for this type of work.

Here is a homemade radiation detector you can build yourself in an evening. The Geiger tube is fragile; be careful with it and use your ingenuity to install it so that it is protected. It can be placed inside an aluminum box, since gamma rays, which are what we are looking for, will pass through aluminum.

To use the radiation finder, a set of high-impedance earphones will be needed. Plug these into jack M3. Hold a radium-dial clock or watch near the Geiger tube. The clicking rate which you hear normally will increase. This is what you should hear when the Geiger tube is held close to ore samples that radiate gamma rays. See Fig. 86 and Table 86.

Table 86. Parts List for Radiation Finder.

Item No.	Description
C1	.01 .μF capacitor.
B1	300-volt battery.
B2	1.5-volt battery.
M1	Output jack 2007
Q1	SK3004 transistor.
Q2	2N228 transistor.
R1, R3	2meg resistor.
R2	30k resistor.
S1	Dpst switch.
V1	1B86 Geiger tube.

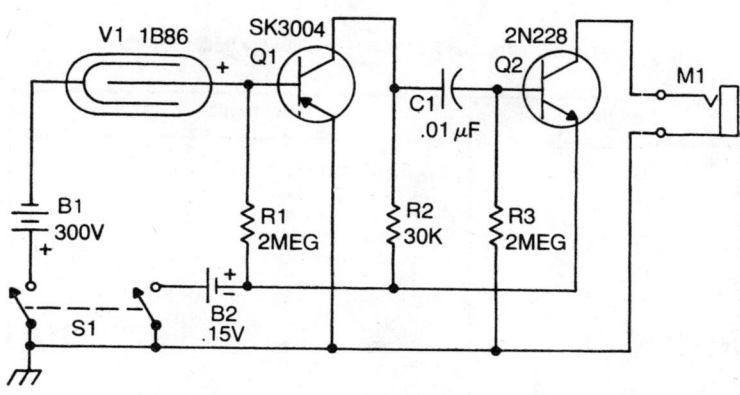

Fig. 86. Radiation finder circuit.

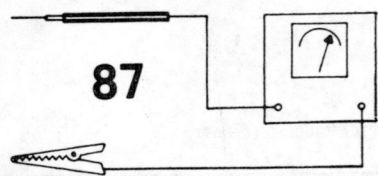

87

Universal Two-Way Radio Tester

As the name implies, this test unit is almost universal. As you can see from studying the schematic, it is a field-strength meter, modulation monitor, and code monitor.

When the unit is used as a modulation monitor, your antenna is a length of insulated wire inside your transmitter enclosure. Start with a short length, as too much rf will burn out the diodes and meter.

L1 is an 18-turn length of B & W 3015 *Miniconductor* tapped 3 turns in from the end. See Fig. 87 and Table 87.

The speaker is an 8-ohm, type.

You will note that there is no battery; none is required. It operates by rectifying the rf from your transmitter.

Table 87. Parts List for Universal Two-Way Radio Tester.

Item No.	Description
C1	365-pF variable capacitor.
C2	.001-μF capacitor.
C3	.01-μF capacitor.
C4	.005-μF capacitor.
C5	.02-μF capacitor.
L1	See text.
L2	2.5-mH choke (National R-300 or equiv.).
L3	1-mH choke (National R-300 or equiv.).
M1	0-1 milliammeter.
M2	Phone jack.
Q1	SK3004 transistor.
R1	250k potentiometer.
S1	Spst switch.
T1	Output transformer: 10,000 ohms, center-tapped push/pull plates to 8-ohm voice coil (Allied Radio No. 54B2363 or equiv.).
X1, X2	1N38B diode.
SP1	8-ohm Speaker.

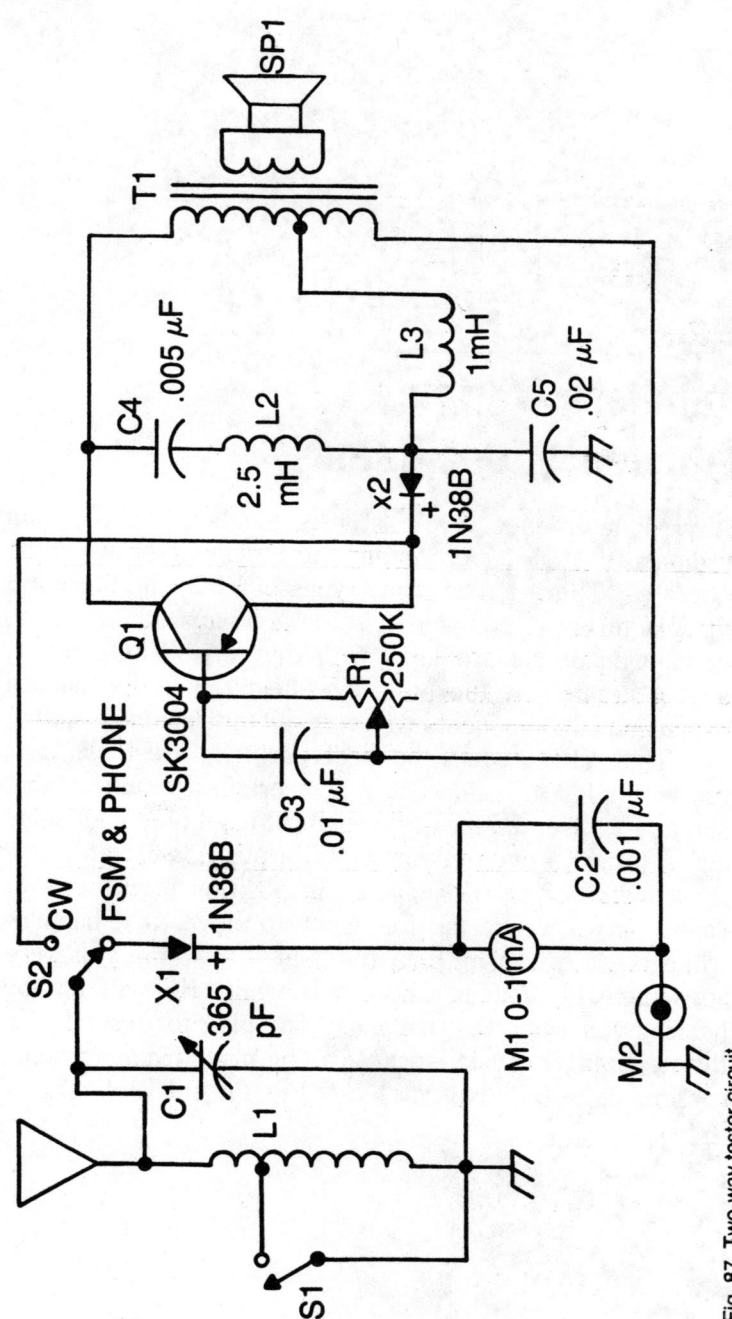

Fig. 87. Two-way tester circuit.

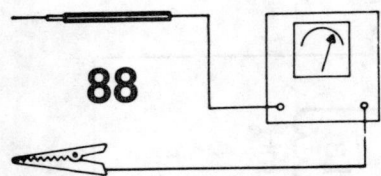

Tubeless Variable Frequency Oscillator

A variable frequency oscillator is the heart of the ham radioman's gear. It determines the frequency on which he operates. There are as many types of VFO's as there are manufacturers of equipment, some good and others not so good. One of the problems with tube type VFO's is the heat generated by the tube. The heat causes mechanical expansion of components with a resultant frequency shift.

This VFO avoids the heat problem. Besides, it is much simpler to build. There are certain precautions that should be observed for best results. Mount all components so as to avoid even minor shifts in position. Even a few thousandths of an inch change in position of the coil or capacitor will cause the frequency to move. If it happens while you are transmitting, the ham with whom you were speaking will wonder where you went. He will not be hearing you when that happens. The plug for inserting in the transmitter crystal socket can be made from a defunct crystal holder (FT-243 type). See Fig. 88 and Table 88.

Table 88. Parts List for Tubeless Variable Frequency Oscillator.

Item No.	Description
	80 Meters
C1	365-pF broadcast variable capacitor.
C2	500-pF silver mica capacitor.
C3	.0025-μF mica capacitor.
L1	32 turns of No. 20 wire, 1-inch diameter, 2 inches long (Air Dux 816T or equiv.).
M1	Two-terminal plug (Mosley 301 or equiv. see text).
	40 Meters
C1	100-pF miniature variable capacitor (Allied Radio No. 43B3756 or equiv.).
C2	300-pF silver mic capacitor.
C3	.0025-μF mica capacitor.
L1	19 turns of No. 20 wire, 1-inch diameter, 1 3/16 inches long (Air Dux 816T or equiv.).
M1	Two-terminal plug (Mosley 301 or equiv. see text).

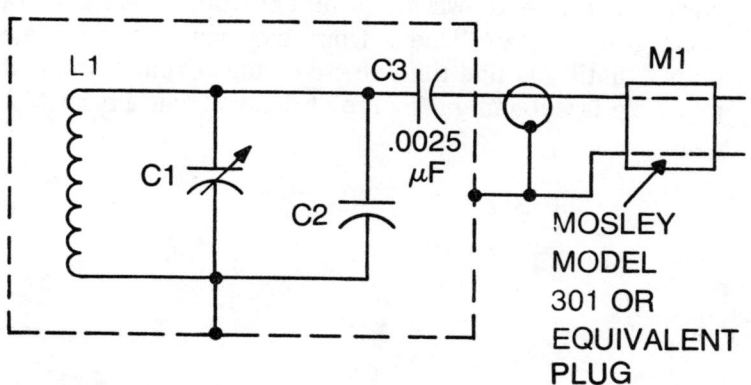

Fig. 88. Variable frequency oscillator circuit.

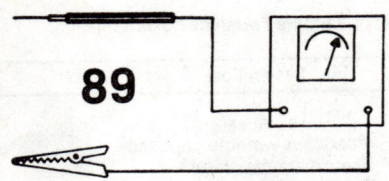

Simple Signal Tracer

A very simple signal tracer can be made as indicated in the schematic. It may be plugged into any audio amplifier, for instance, your record player or hi-fi unit. The output end must be equipped with a plug to suit the jack on your audio amplifier.

The probe pin must be insulated from the metal shell as indicated. Make the ground lead about 18 inches long and attach an alligator clip. See Fig. 89 and Table 89.

To use, warm up the audio amplifier and plug in the signal tracer. Next, warm up the unit to be tested. Work from grid to plate leads, from the input towards the output, until you find the defective stage. Your audio unit may help in detecting a source of distortion at a particular stage.

Table 89. Parts List for Simple Signal Tracer.

Item No.	Description
C1	.001-μF, 600-volt capacitor.
X1	1N38B diode.

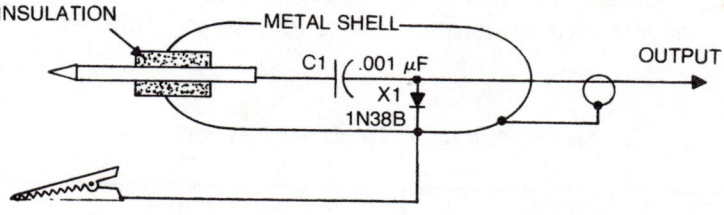

Fig. 89. Signal tracer circuit.

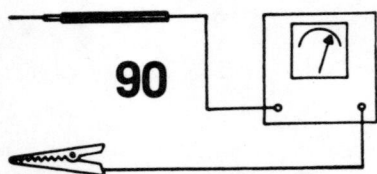

Variable Bench-Voltage Supply

Most of us have been putting together various experimental transistorized devices for some time. These work fine on batteries, but after a while it is realized that a variable voltage supply is a lot more convenient and, certainly, less expensive than batteries.

Here is a simple unit which can be used from 0 voltage to 25 volts and with up to about 500 milliamps. You will find the components are not expensive. The SK3009 transistor is quite rugged and can be overloaded somewhat without ill effects. See Fig. 90 and Table 90.

Table 90. Parts List for Variable Bench-Voltage Supply.

Item No.	Description
C1, C2	500-μF, 15-volt electrolytic capacitors.
Q1	SK3009 transistor.
R1	750-ohm, 5-watt potentiometer.
R2	100-ohm, 10-watt resistor.
R3	200-ohm, 10-watt resistor.
T1	26.5-volt filament transformer .6 A (Allied Radio No. 54B1476 or equiv.).
X1, X2	Rectifiers (GE-504A or equiv.).

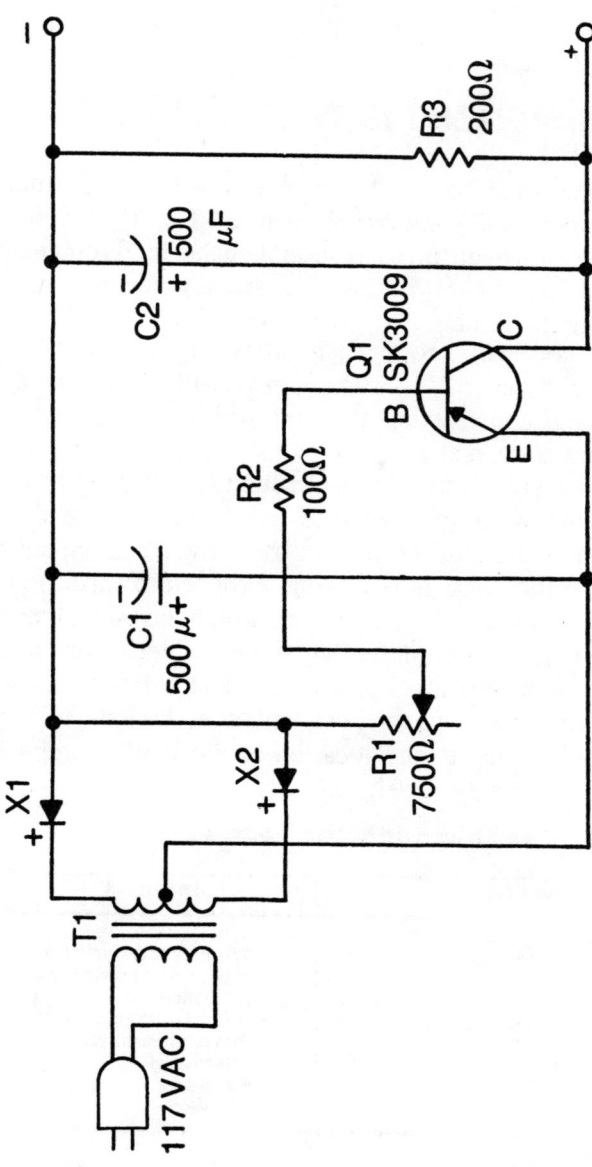

Fig. 90. Variable-voltage supply circuit.

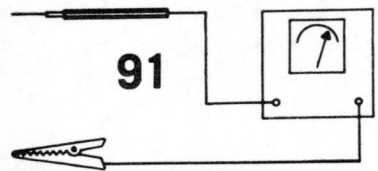

Transistorized Injector Probe

This transistorized injector probe is a neat little multivibrator operating somewhere near 5 kHz. Harmonics are readable, however, up to several megahertz. Troubleshooting of hi-fi amplifiers, radios, TV, etc. is made easy with the aid of this little unit.

As you will see from a study of the diagram, the circuit is simple. The components will cost only a few dollars and constructing the unit will give you a pleasant few hours of relaxation.

To use this unit, clip the ground lead to the chassis or bus ground of the unit being tested. Start at the grid of the last tube or the base of the last transistor. You should hear a sound if the stage is operating. Proceed toward the front end until you reach a stage at which no signal can be heard. This is the defective stage. Check for shorted capacitors or open resistors. A check of the operating voltages of the stage or resistances at various tube pins will supply clues to the location of the faulty component. See Fig. 91 and Table 91.

Table 91. Parts List for Transistorized Injector Probe.

Item No.	Description
C1, C2	.005-μF, disc ceramic capacitors.
C3	120-pF, disc ceramic capacitor.
B1	4-volt battery.
Q1, Q2	2N228 transistors.
R1, R5	1880-ohm resistors.
R2, R6	43-ohm resistors.
R3, R4	30k resistors.
S1	Spst switch.

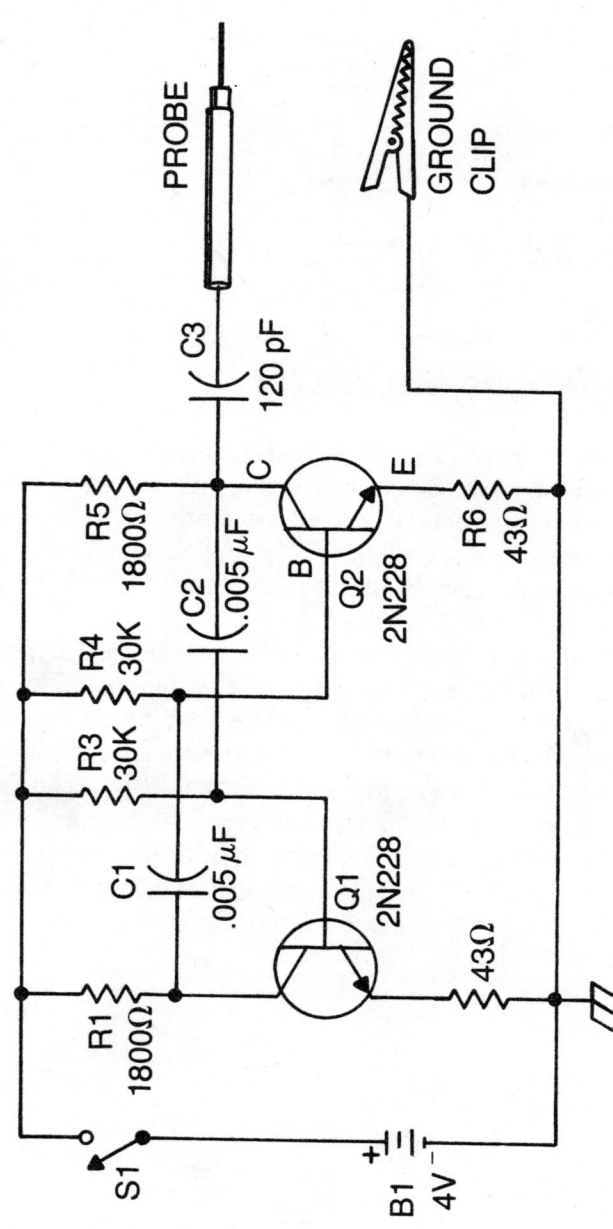

Fig. 91. Injector probe circuit.

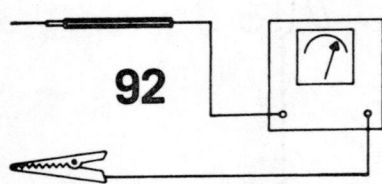

Grid Dipper Modulator

Many of you have available a grid dip meter, a very useful item of test gear. Since a grid dip meter covers a very broad range of frequencies and generates an rf signal, it can be used as a signal generator but you will require a method of adding modulation to the rf coming from the grid dipper.

Here is an easy way to do it. You even use power from the grid dipper. The parts cost is minimal. The unit is designed to plug into the phone jack of the grid dip meter and takes its power to drive the transistor from the grid dipper. The transformer T1 serves as an audio feedback connector between the collector and emitter of Q1, the SK3004 transistor. The oscillation of the transistor is impressed on the rf signal of the grid dip meter and you are in business with a modulated signal generator. See Fig. 92 and Table 92.

Table 92. Parts List for Grid Dipper Modulator.

Item No.	Description
C1	.015-μF, 100-volt capacitor.
M1	Phone plug.
Q1	SK3004 transistor.
R1	1.1k resistor.
T1	Transistor transformer (Lafayette Radio No. TR-98 or equiv.).

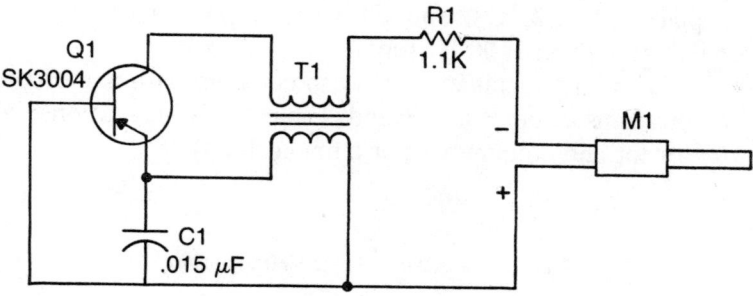

Fig. 92. Grid dipper modulator circuit.

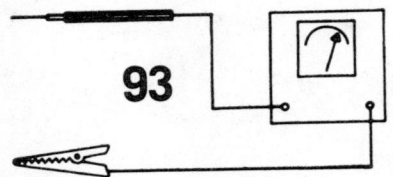

Simple Phase-Shift Oscillator

Transistor phase-shift oscillators are little-known jewels of design to the experimenter who really wants to experiment. The unit shown in the accompanying diagram, for example, produces a clean sine wave and starts easily every time it is put into operation. Most important, it will continue oscillating long after battery voltage has dropped significantly below the recommended 12 Vdc.

Uses? Unlimited! As shown here, the shifter will produce a clear 2100-Hz tone with parts specified. If you change capacitor values (*not* the resistors), you can appreciably affect resultant tone. For example, you can replace C1, C2, C3, and C4 with .1 μF capacitors and wind up with an 1100-Hz tone.

With any imagination you can come up with numerous applications. See Fig. 93 and Table 93. (Suggestions: a tester for audio equipment or a musical toy).

Table 93. Parts List for Phase-Shift Oscillator.

Item No.	Description
C1, C2, C3, C4	.068-μF capacitors.
B1	12-volt battery.
Q1	2N270 transistor.
R1	5.6k, 2-watt resistor.
R2, R3, R4	680-ohm, 2-watt resistors.
R5	68k, 2-watt resistor.
R6	1.2k, 2-watt resistor.
S1	Spst switch.

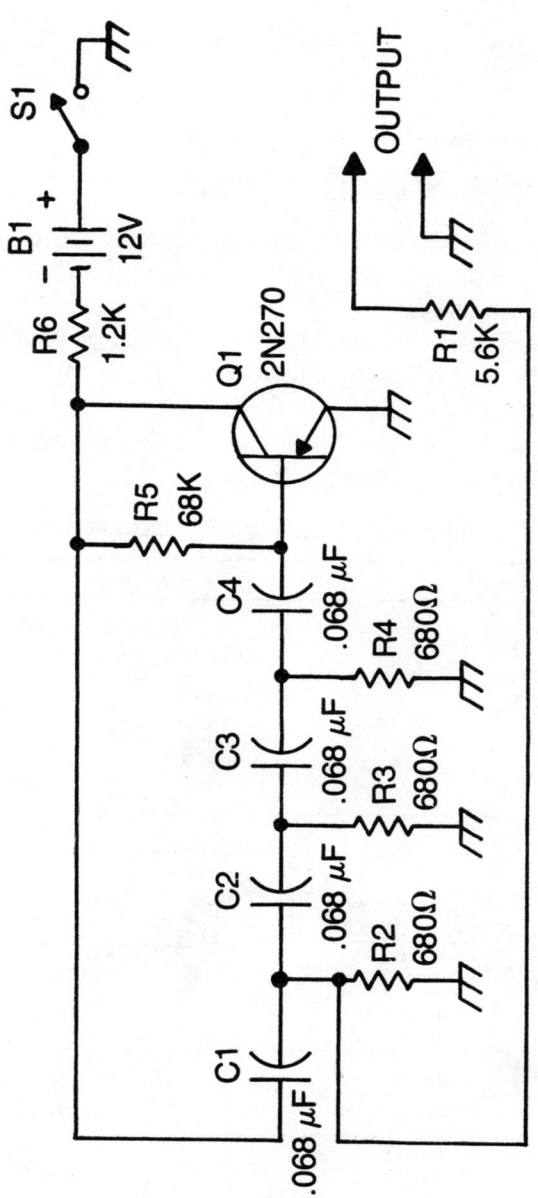

Fig. 93. Phase-shift oscillator circuit.

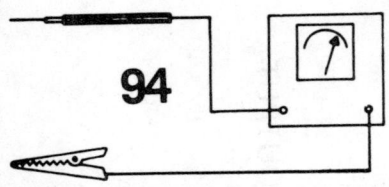

One-Tube Signal Injector

Here is a line-powered signal injector you can use for rf circuits as well as audio circuits. Use it on either rf or i-f stages, as you wish.

This circuit is isolated from the case. For your safety, be sure the two grounds shown are made to the case. See Fig. 94 and Table 94.

You will find this little signal injector one of your most useful pieces of test gear.

Table 94. Parts List for One-Tube Signal Injector.

Item No.	Description
C1,C3,C4	.015-µF disc ceramic capacitors
C2	.0047-µF disc ceramic capacitor.
R1	1k, 5-watt resistor.
R2,R3	51k resistors.
R4,R5	11k resistors.
R6	910-ohm resistor.
S1	Spst switch.
V1	6060 tube.

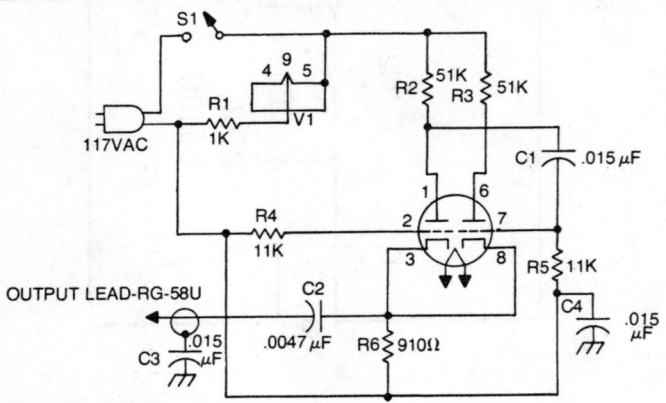

Fig. 94. Signal injector circuit.

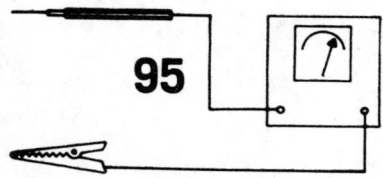

Direct-Current Controller

A direct-current controller is a very handy unit to own. If you build it yourself you will understand how it works and will be able to readily perform any service required. Model railroading or model building makes it desirable to have a variable-voltage dc supply. Any dc supply of not more than 15 to 16 volts will serve as the input.

R2 is the variable-voltage controller and can be set to any amount up to full voltage. See Fig. 95 and Table 95.

Table 95. Parts List for Direct-Current Controller.

Item No.	Description
F1	1.5-A circuit breaker (Allied Radio No. 57B3577 or equiv.).
Q1	SK3009 transistor.
R1	160-ohm, 2-watt resistor.
R2	750-ohm, 5-watt potentiometer.

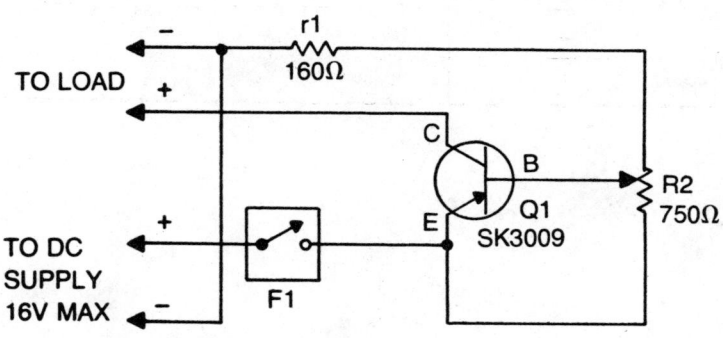

Fig. 95. Direct-current controller circuit.

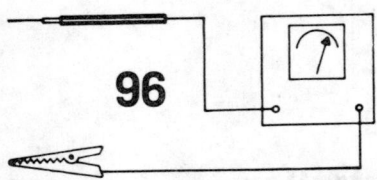

Versatile $1.99 Tester

Do not let the simplicity of this circuit fool you. This tester has many uses. Perhaps you will think of some new ones.

In essence, this is a continuity tester with its own power source. To use it, connect it to the component being tested. For instance, to check a rectifier, connect the tester to the two terminals and close the switch. If the light M1 glows, reverse the leads and try again. The rectifier is bad if the light glows when connected both ways.

You may use this device to check continuity. You have electrical continuity as long as the light glows. See Fig. 96 and Table 96.

Table 96. Parts List for Versatile $1.99 Tester.

Item No.	Description
B1	Two 9-volt transistor radio batteries in series.
M1	No. 49 pilot light.
R1	110-ohm resistor.
S1	Spst switch.

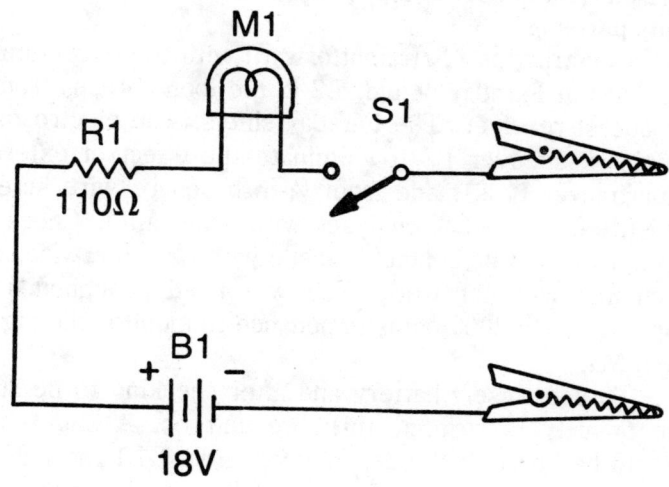

Fig. 96. Versatile tester circuit.

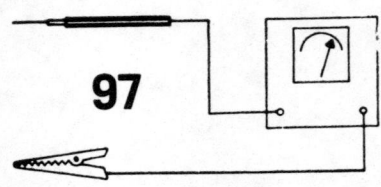

Metal Locator

Did you ever feel the need for a practical metal detector? Here is a lightweight, easy-to-build unit that will find buried pipes, conduit, plumbing, etc. The unit is transistorized, and is operated by a single 15-volt battery so it is truly portable.

Construction is straightforward with the exception of L2 and the Faraday shield. L2 is the loop antenna from a broadcast receiver. The Faraday shield is an electrostatic shield, used over L2 to eliminate the effect of external capacitance. It is made from ¼-inch square wire screen and fitted over L2 (see inset with schematic). Check to make sure that no contact is made with L2, otherwise, the oscillator will not work. You will need headphones of approximately 2000-ohms impedance to monitor the signal from M1.

To use, insert battery and after checking to be sure the polarity is correct, turn the unit on. A slight hiss should be heard in the headphones. Adjust L1 through its range to see if a beat is heard. If none is heard, try changing the value of C8 to a greater or lesser value. As indicated, R5 should be adjusted until a growl is heard in the earphones.

In use, when the loop is brought near a metallic object, the tone heard in the phones will change in pitch. See Fig. 97 and Table 97.

Table 97. Parts List for Metal Locator.

Item No.	Description
C1, C4	100-pF capacitors.
C2, C5, C6, C7, C10	.005-µF capacitors.
C3	470-pF capacitor.
C8	.005µF capacitor.
C9	.1-µF capacitor.
L1	Loopstick antenna.
L2	A-m broadcast loop antenna.
B1	15-volt battery.
M1	Insulated phone jack.
Q1, Q2, Q3	SK3004 transistors.
R1, R3	7.5k resistors.
R2, R4	270k resistors.
R5	1k potentiometer.
R6	6.2k resistor.
R7	470k resistor.
S1	Spst switch.

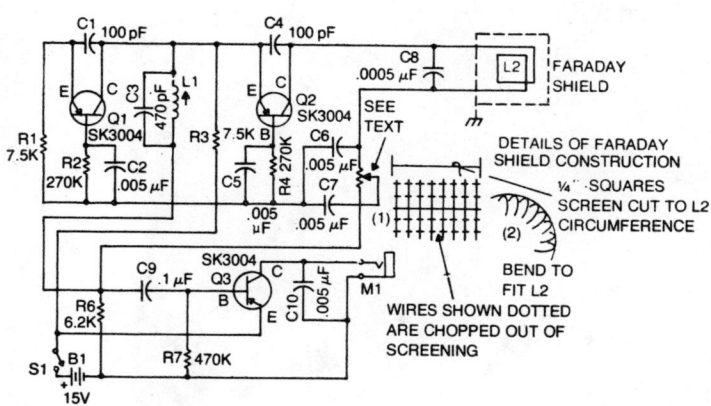

Fig. 97. Metal locator circuit.

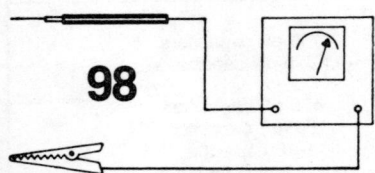

Capacitor Tester For VOM's

Most of us know that capacitors pass ac but block dc voltage. We can put that fact to use to help us to measure capacitors.

A setup is made with your vacuum-type voltmeter and 117 Vac current. As the diagram indicates, it is simple, *but do it safely*. Connect the capacitor to be tested as shown. Throw the switch and read the voltage shown on your VOM. Refer to Table 98A for the capacitor size that agrees with the indicated voltage. See Fig. 98 and Tables 98A and 98B.

Table 98A. Parts List for Capacitor Tester for VOMs.

Item No.	Description
C1	.5-μF, 500-volt capacitor.
S1	Spst switch.

Table 98B. Capacitor Values.

Ac Volts	Microfarads	Ac Volts	Microfarads
75	.10	8	.04
65	.8	4	.02
57	.6	2	.01
45	.4	1.6	.008
30	.2	1.3	.006
17	.1	.8	.004
14	.08	.4	.002
10	.05	.2	.001

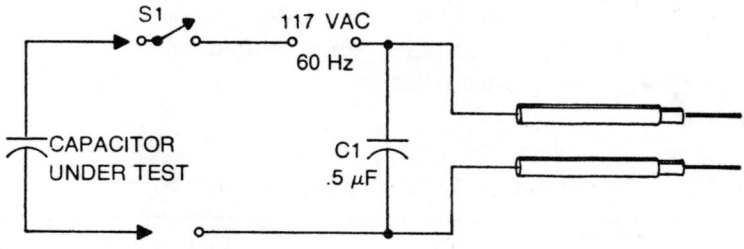

Fig. 98. Capacitor tester circuit.

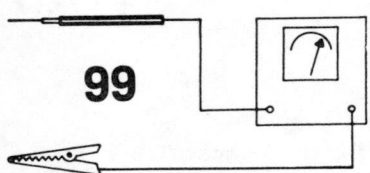

High-Voltage Converter For Your Battery

For those of you who will want a high-voltage source that can be operated from a 12-volt battery, here is just the thing for you. This unit will deliver 250 to 275 volts at 125 milliamperes for your needs. It is just the thing to supply power to drive a low-to-medium power mobile ham transmitter.

The transistors used here should be mounted directly on the chassis. The insulated washers will transmit heat to the chassis. *There should be no electrical connection to the chassis.* Check this with an ohmmeter after construction. Go over the wiring for correctness and use your ohmmeter to make certain you have not made any mistake before applying power. See Fig. 99 and Table 99.

If you happen to need a 6-volt filament supply, connect a 2-0hm, 25-watt resistor in series with the 12-volt lead.

Table 99. Parts List for High-Voltage Converter for Your Battery.

Item No.	Description
C1	50-μF, 450-volt electrolytic capacitor.
Q1, Q2	SK3009 transistors.
R1	1.3-ohm, 2-watt resistor.
R2	200-ohm, 5-watt resistor.
R3	110k, 2-watt resistor.
T1	Transistor power transformer: primary, 117 Vac; secondary 280 Vac, 125 mA (Chicago Transformer DCT-1 or equiv.).
X1, X2, X3, X4	Diodes (GE-504A or equiv.).

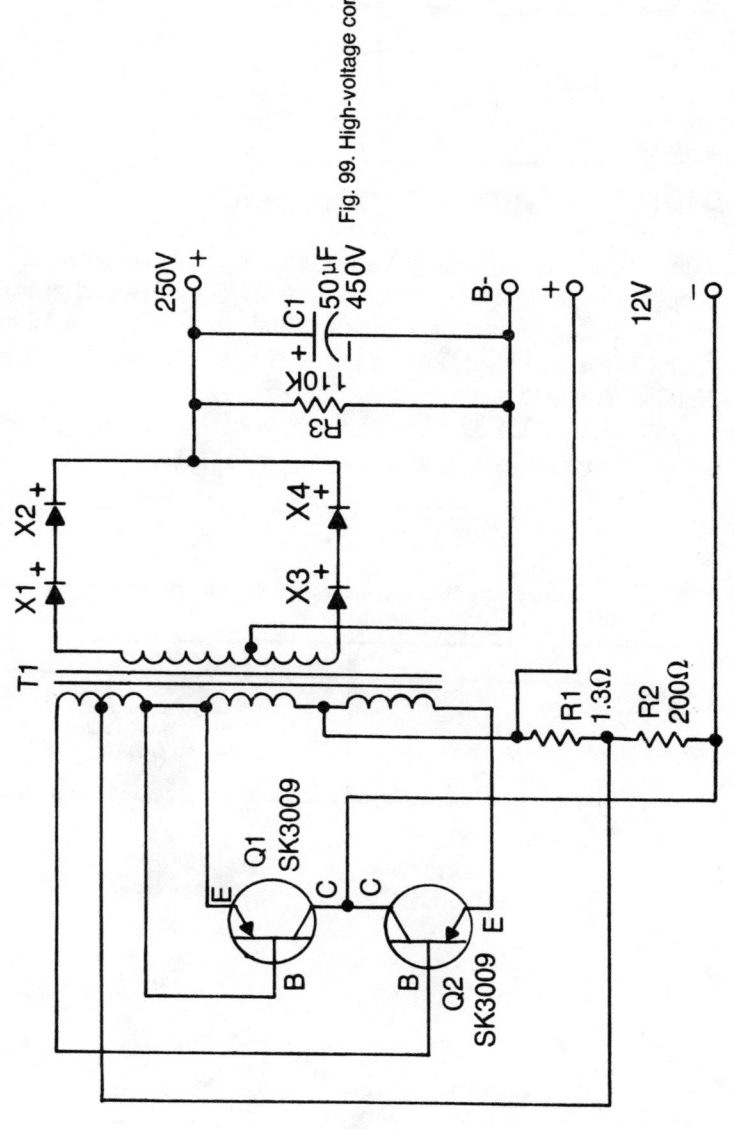

Fig. 99. High-voltage converter circuit.

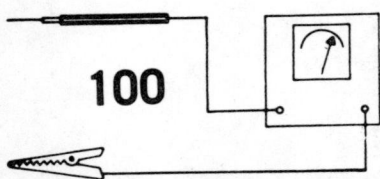

Antenna Current Indicator

This little unit will show you whether your transmitter is properly loaded by the antenna. Connect between transmitter and antenna and adjust final tuning and loading controls for maximum brilliance of the lamps. See Fig. 100 and Table 100.

Capacitor C1 is sized for a 70-watt rig. For lower-powered rigs, use a smaller capacitor for C1.

Table 100. Parts List for Antenna Current Indicator.

Item No.	Description
C1	.01-μF capacitor.
M1, M2	RCA phone jacks.
M3, M4, M5, M6	No. 46 pilot lamps.

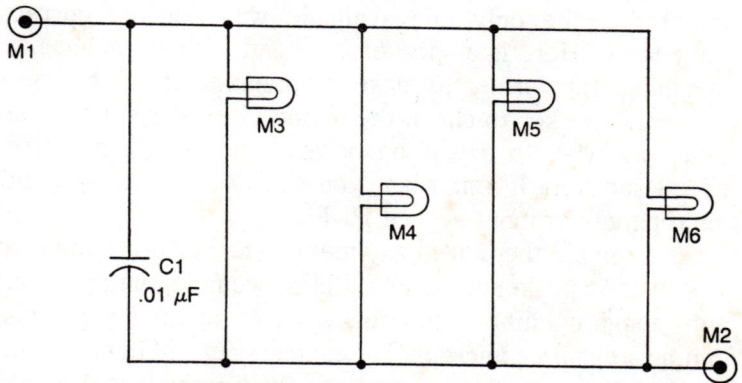

Fig. 100. Antenna current indicator circuit.

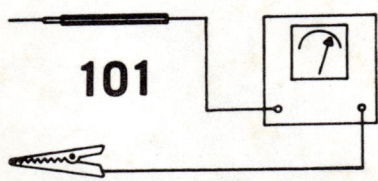

Universal Test Speaker

You may have needed a speaker for test purposes and found that the only one available was not the correct impedance. Here is a speaker arranged with an impedance matching transformer to make it universal. It can be used as a test speaker to check the action of existing speakers. You may wish to use it on occasion as an extension or added speaker. If you wish, you can use it as a dynamic microphone for input to your Hi-Fi.

    Assemble the unit in any metal box. Perforate the box where the speaker is mounted. Use your ingenuity here; not enough openings will affect speaker sound. To use this unit as a dynamic microphone, connect jacks M1 and M3 to the input of a tube-type amplifier (high impedance). Connect jacks M4 and M5 if the amplifier is a transistor type (low impedance).

    To use as a test speaker, connect terminals M4 and M5 in parallel with the speaker being tested. Select the transformer terminals that produce the best results. See Fig. 101 and Table 101.

Table 101. Parts List for Universal Test Speaker.

Item No.	Description
M1, M2, M3, M4, M5	Tip jacks.
T1	Universal output transformer: push/pull plates to voice coil (Allied Radio No. 54B2023 or equiv.).
SP1	4" to 10" speaker.

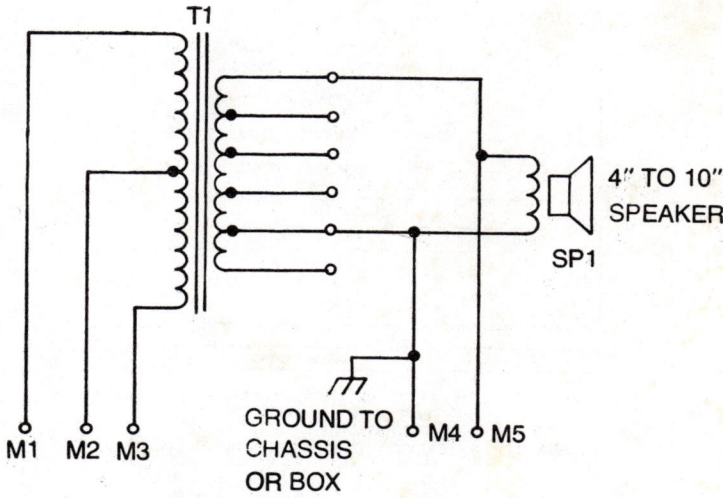

Fig. 101. Universal test speaker circuit.

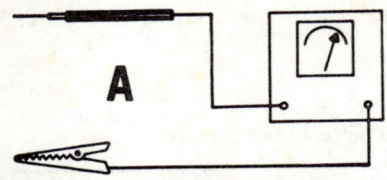

Substitution Guide

The listings that follow are standard substitutions for most of the diodes, tubes, and transistors used in projects in this book. These replacements have not been used in the circuits and therefore some performance changes should be anticipated by the constructor, although these variances will be slight. Where no substitution is given, no practical one was found.

It should be indicated that the general replacement transistor types manufactured by the various companies are special in that they are *universal* transistor substitutes. Therefore, a single GE-2, for example, replaces *hundreds* of conventional transistor types. For this reason, we have indicated only a small percentage of these universal replacements in this listing. For complete cross-reference sheets, contact your local radio parts outlet.

Transistors

Transistor	Substitute
SK3004	2N192, DS26, AA1, 2N415, CK722, GE-2, 20V-MG, 2N466, 2N109
SK3009	2N255, 2N555, 2N376A, GE-3, 2N554, 2N256
2N228	2N35, 2N385A, 2N1299, 2N1605A
SK3011	2N94A, 2N168A, 2N170, GE-7, NR5, TR-10, DS75, TR-59
SK3003	2N138, 2N138A, TR-05, DS26, 2N711, 2N711A, 2N535B, 2N536
2N109	SK3004, CK722, GE-2, 20V-MG, 2N466
2N466	2SB265, 40269, 2N109, 2SB416, SK3004, B5M, GE-2
2N228	2N35, 2N385A, 2N1299, 2N1605A, GE-8, NR5, TR-09, DS66, AA2, TR-60, SK7
2N525	2N43, 2N43A, 2N526, 2N650, 2N650A, 2N1057, 30V-LG
SK3008	2N1631, 2N1632, 2N1635, 2N1636, 2N1637, GE-1, BE6

Diodes

Diode	Substitute
1N38B	1N34A, 1N34, DN34A, 1N38
1N60	1N295, DN295
1N118	1N54A, 1N54
1N34A	1N38, 1N38B, 1N34, DN34A

Tubes

Tube	Substitute
6100	6C4
6060	12AT7, 12AT7WA, 12AT7WB, 6201, 6671, 6679, 7492, 7728
117P7	117N7, 117N7-GT
6EA8	6AX8, 6GH8, 6LN8, 6U8, 6U8A, 1252, 6678, 7731
5U4G	5AR4, 5AS4, 5AS4A, 5AU4, 5DB4, 5R4, 5T4, 5U4GA, 5U4GB, 5V4, 524, 5931, 6087, 6106
5963	12AU7, 12AU7A, 12AU7W, 12AU7WA, 6067, 6189, 6680, 7316, 7489, 7730

Appendix B
Resistor Color Codes

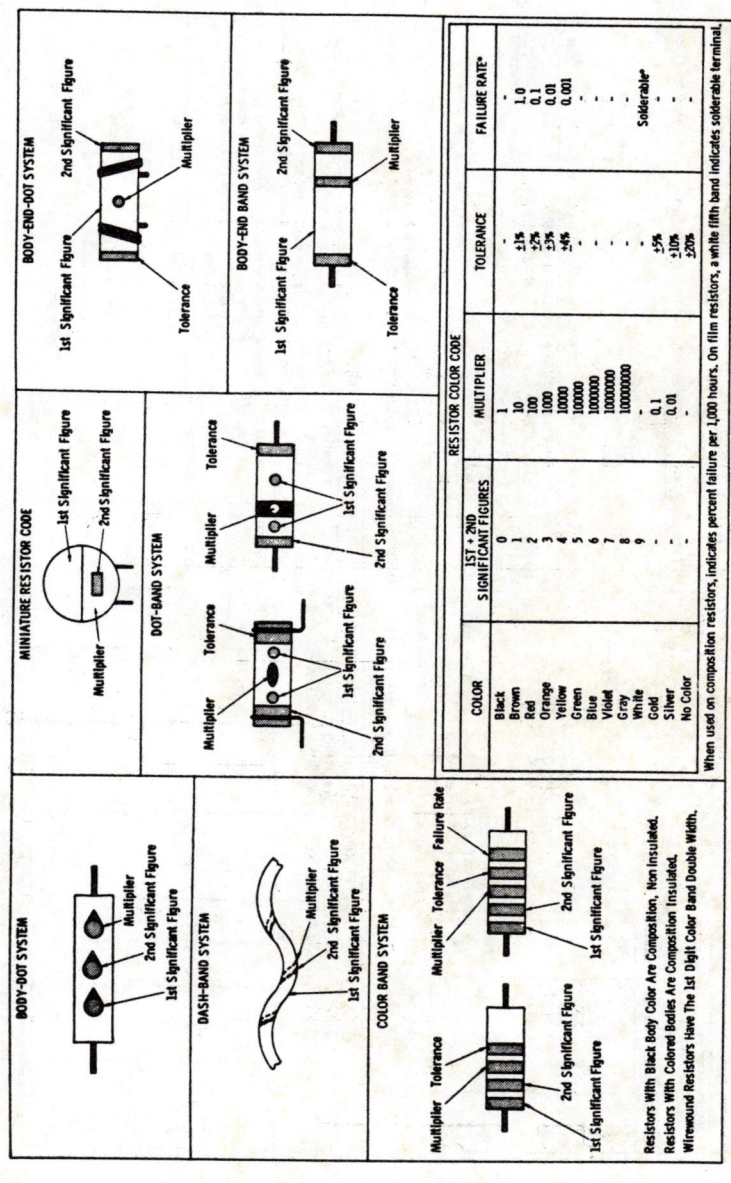

Appendix C

Capacitor Color Codes

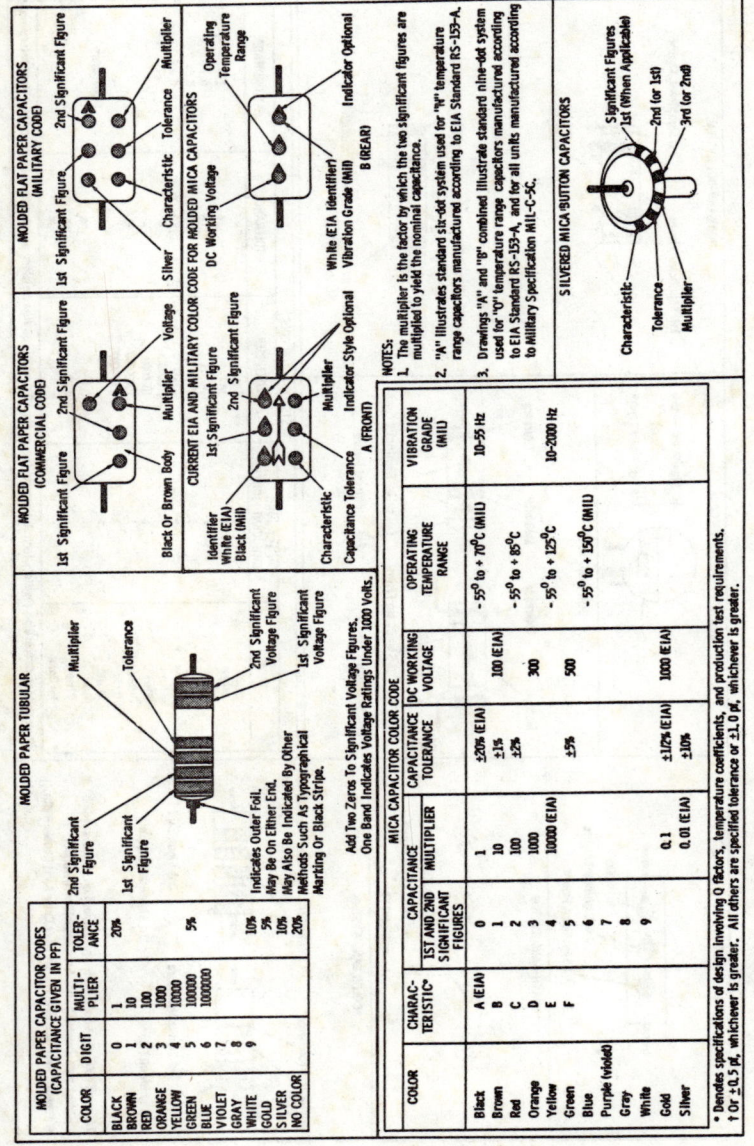

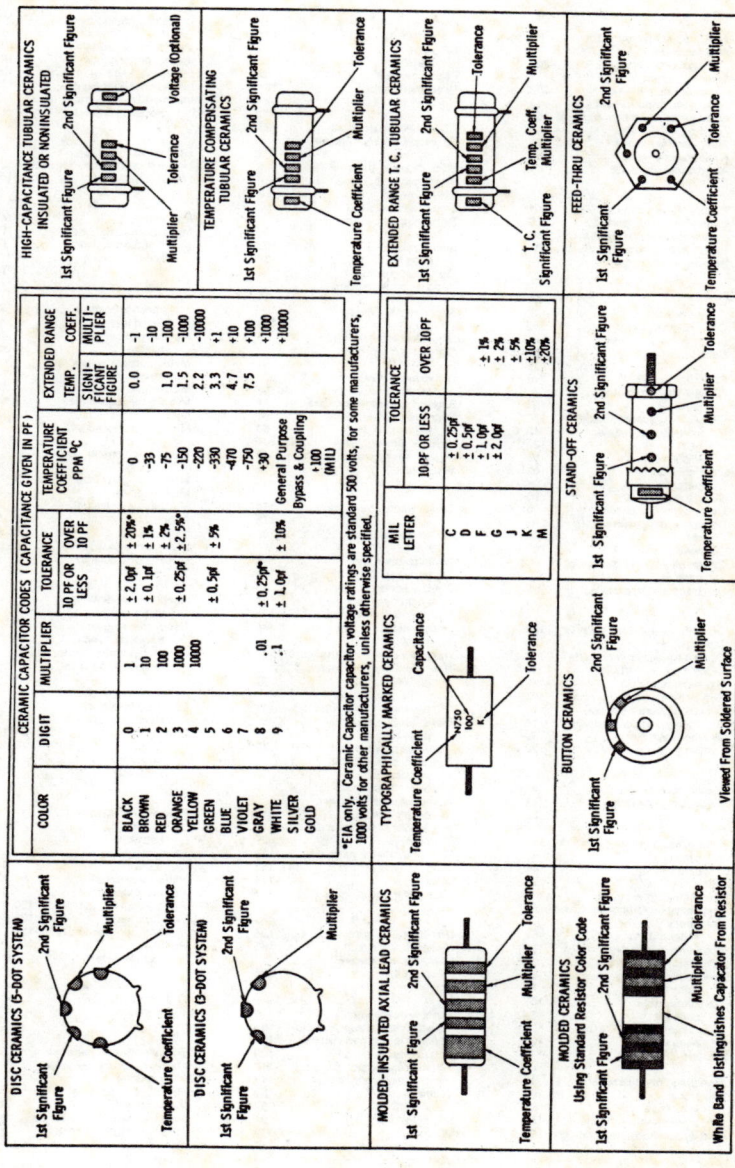

Index

A

AC-DC voltmeter, parts list	83
Antenna current dindicator circuit	203
Antenna current indicator, parts list	202
Astable multivibrator, parts list	45
Audio frequency meter, parts list	65
Audio oscillator circuit	47
Audio oscillator, parts list	46, 127
Audio tracer circuit	147
Audio tracer, parts list	147

B

Battery converter circuit	201
Battery converter, parts list	200
Battery rejuvenator, parts list	93
Bench-voltage supply, parts list	184
Booster, line-voltage	26

C

Calibrator	86, 136, 156
parts list	137
Capacitor leakage checker, parts list	121
Capacitor tester	90, 198
parts list	91, 199
Capacitor values	199
CB field strength meter, parts list	55
Checker, capacitor leakage	120
intermediate-frequency	42
SCR	122
silicon rectifier	50
transistor	96, 106
Comparator	94
Comparator circuit	95
Continuity tester circuit	9
Controller, direct-current	193
unit	134
Converter	200
Crystal microphone substitute, parts list	39
Crystal oscillator, parts list	165

D

DC motor supply unit, parts list	153
Detector	74
Diode frequency meter, parts list	117
Diode rf probe, parts list	53
Dip meter, parts list	169
Direct-current controller circuit	193
Dry cell rejuvenator circuit	15
Dry cell rejuvenator, parts list	14
Dynamic mike circuit	33
Dynamic mike, parts list	32

E

Electronic timer, parts list	41
Expander, VOM range	13

F

Field strength meter	54, 144
circuit	55, 145
parts list	144
Filter	128
Frequency meter circuit	117
Frequency meter/monitor circuit	67
Frequency meter/monitor, parts list	66
Frequency oscillator, parts list	181
Frequency standard circuit	37, 77
Frequency standard, one-tube	36
transistor	76
Fuse indicator,	160
parts list	161
Fuse saver	104
parts list	105

G

Generator, neon-lamp tone	30
signal	62, 166
sine-wave	10, 58
square-wave	148
Grid dipper modulator, parts list	189

H

Household wattmeter, parts list	12

I

Impedance checker	
20 parts list	21

Rf meter	24
parts list	171
RF probe	18
parts list	19
Rf probe circuit	53
Rf voltmeter circuit	171

S

SCR checker, parts list	123
Shockless continuity tester, part list	9
Short detector, parts list	75
Signal generator, parts list	63, 167
Signal injector	192
Signal injector circuit	192
Signal strength meter, parts list	99
Signal tracer	70, 78, 102
parts list	103, 183
Signal tracer circuit	71
Silicon rectifier checker parts list	51
Silicon rectifier tester, parts list	109
Signal tracer circuit	79
Signal-injector probe, parts list	151
Sine-wave generator, parts list	10, 59
Sine-wave generator circuit	11
Sound level meter, circuit	61
parts list	60
Speaker, universal test	204
Square-wave generator circuit	149
Supply unit	152

T

Tester, neon-lamp polarity	154
radio	178
silicon rectifier	108
transistor	174
Tester/charger, cell	112
parts list	113
Timer, electronic	40
Tone generator circuit	31
Tool magnetizer, parts list	141
Tracer, audio	146
signal	182
Transistor checker, parts list	97, 107
Transistor frequency standard, parts list	77
Transistor metronome, parts list	111
Transistor power supply, parts list	35
Transistor power supply circuit	17
Transistor signal tracer, parts list	70
Transistor tester, parts list	175
Transistor variable power supply parts list	16
Transistorized moisturemeter, parts list	29
Tube rejuvenator, parts list	162
Tube rejuvenator circuit	101, 163
Tube tester	114
Tube tester circuit	115

U

Unit controller, parts list	134
Unit controller circuit	135
Universal test speaker, parts list	205

V

Variable power supply	16
Variable-voltage supply circuit	185
Versatile tester, parts list	184
Versatile tester circuit	195
Vibrator rejuvenator, parts list	142
Vibrator rejuvenator circuit	143
Voltmeter	80
AC-DC	82
Voltmeter circuit	81
VOM	118
parts list	119
VOM circuit	119
VOM range expander, part list	13
VOM Rf indicator, parts list	49

W

Wattmeter	12

Indicator, antenna current	202
rf	48
Injector probe, parts list	186
Injector probe circuit	187
Interference filter, parts list	128
Interference filter circuit	129
Intermediate-frequency checker, parts list	43

L

Light meter, parts list	73
Line-voltage booster, parts list	27
Locator, metal	196

M

Magnetizer	140
Metal locator, parts list	197
Meter, audio frequency	64
diode frequency	116
dip	168
light	72
rf	170
signal-strength	98
sound level	60
Meter sensitizer	68
parts list	69
Meter/monitor, frequency	66
Metronome, transistor	110
Microphone circuit	39
Microphone, substitute	38
Mike	32
Miniature power supply, parts list	57
Miniature voltmeter, parts list	81
Modulator, grid dipper	188
Moisturemeter	28
Moisturemeter circuit	29
Multitester	84, 88
parts list	85, 89
Multitester circuit	85, 89
Multivibrator, astable	44

N

Neon-lamp polarity tester, parts list	155
Neon-lamp singnal tracer, parts list	79
Neon-lamp tone generator, parts list	31

O

One-tube frequency standard, parts list	37
Oscillator	138, 164, 190
audio	46, 126
frequency	180
parts list	139

P

Phase-shift oscillator circuit	191
parts list	190
Photo relay	132
parts list	132
Photo relay circuit	133
Polarity tester circuit	155
Power supply	22, 34, 56, 130, 158
parts list	23, 130, 158
Power supply circuit	35, 131, 159
Probe, rf	52
signal-injector	150

Q

Q-multiplier	172
parts list	173

R

Radiation finder, parts list	177
Radio frequency calibrator, parts list	87
Radio tester, parts list	178
Radio tester circuit	179
Receiver calibrator, parts list	175
Receiver calibrator circuit	137
Rejuvenator	92, 142
parts list	101
tube	100, 162
Rf, indicate	124
parts list	124
Rf indicator, circuit	125
Rf indicator circuit	49

Edited by Roland S. Phelps